BUILDING
FREE-FORM
FURNITURE

BUILDING
FREE-FORM
FURNITURE

BY CHARLES W. DURNEY

TAB BOOKS Inc.

BLUE RIDGE SUMMIT, PA. 17214

684.104

FIRST EDITION

FIRST PRINTING

Copyright © 1982 by TAB BOOKS Inc.

Printed in the United States of America

Library of Congress Cataloging in Publication Data

Durney, Charles W.
    Building free-form furniture.

    Includes index.
    1. Furniture making. I. Title.
TT194.D87 1982   684.1′04   82-5827
ISBN 0-8306-1340-4   AACR2
ISBN 0-8306-1440-0 (pbk.)

Contents

Preface

Mother Nature is a generous giver and, at the same time, a cruel tantalizer. She offers breathtaking sights—like a sunset over a bay or mountains—and, as we are savoring the everchanging delight, she gently and quietly fades it from our vision. Even a camera cannot capture the total involvement we feed at that moment. Yet one of the magnificent aspects of nature is that it is ever-changing, ever new. She always offers something to replace what she has snatched away. She is aware of the needs of her children, the needs to possess, and the need for some permanence. She doesn't spoil us by handing us expensive things and demanding nothing. Here, my child, is a tree. Learn to know it, see what it has to offer, unfold its inner beauty, discover for yourself its personality, work to find the satin grain, the swirls and shades of color that vary with every board and never seem to lose their fascination. This part of me, my child, is yours to enjoy, to admire, to use, to keep, of which to never grow tired.

Acknowledgments

I want to thank the following for their help.

My friends for encouraging me to write this book, and especially Al Fosbenner—who provided the impetus to get me started.

My typists for their patience and hours of work . . . Jeanne, Antoinette, Arlene, Ginny, Bea, Sister Jo-El and her typing class, and the secretaries at school.

Mike Fosbenner who did some of the illustrations.

My friend and consultant on many of these projects, Bill Kilpatrick, whose help and suggestions made this book not only much easier, but also pleasant.

My friend, Bill Katrina, for taking most of the pictures for me in spite of his busy schedule.

Paul Moser, Joe Woodward, and Bob Florig for their help and use of their heavy equipment (saving me many hours of work).

My brother Jack and his wife, Lorrie, for conning me into making two rooms of furniture for their home, and thus providing the subjects for some of the pictures for this book.

And I thank you for having an interest in creating furniture that I feel is simplistically beautiful and practical.

Introduction

Making free-form furniture, remodeling in free form, or just making a few odds and ends to decorate a given area are within the realms of possibility for anyone with basic tools and skills. Free form need not be restricted to use by the professional. My start with free form was prompted by need.

I lived in a two-room apartment and I had no furniture in the living room and no money with which to buy furniture. The price of lumber, at that time, was prohibitive and I could not get aesthetically excited over plain lumber. I decided to cut the raw wood myself and use it in as much of its natural shape as possible. I had never seen free-form furniture. I had never even heard the term *free form*.

I found out later that what I had in mind was termed "free form" or "free edge" or "natural form." This style was growing in popularity and it was very expensive to purchase. In my investigation of such furniture, I found that most of it was walnut, and mostly it was made of 1-inch stock. I saw one couch and chair (without cushions) priced at $1000. A dining table, no chairs, was listed at $1700. Coffee tables were priced from $250.00 up; I have seen them as high as $1000.

Whether you are buying finished free-form furniture, paying for a one-of-a kind unfinished piece of wood requiring much hard work, or buying regular commercial furniture, you might find yourself facing high prices. The retail store marks up its stock nearly 100 percent. Most of the markup is due to overhead for the manufacturer, handlers, drivers, the retailer, salespeople, as well as all the operating expenses. You must also pay the price of an inflationary economy. Bargains are available, but there is some truth in the saying "you get no more than you pay for."

In your residence, you might have to stay with what you have as serviceable or be forced into the unenviable position of trying to blend what you can afford with what you can live with. If you were perfectly happy with secondhand furniture, completely satisfied with what you have, or even quite content with what you can afford to buy new, you would not have picked up this book.

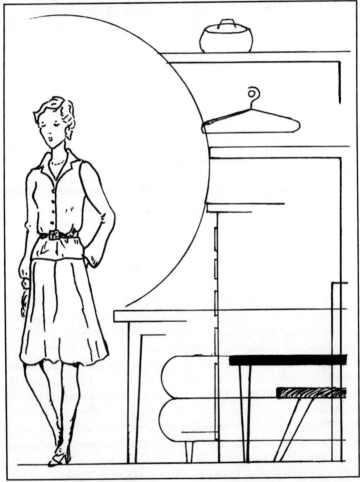

Fig. I-1. Household furniture height compared to the person of average height.

Fig. I-2. Free-form furniture shown in its initial stage.

This book offers techniques for marrying the relatively inexpensive and the naturally beautiful in the world of furniture. Most men and women are capable of building furniture even though some have never tested their latent talents. Worse yet, some will not try because they don't believe the ability is there.

Some people claim they cannot drive a nail straight. Maybe they can't at the start. But if they would hammer a few bags of nails, they would soon learn the technique. I will attempt, in the following pages, to offer some shortcuts that will lessen the demand on expertise, time, effort, and expense.

There is much to be said for taking something from nature, with its own specific beauty, and making it functional. It is often said that beauty is in the eye of the beholder. Yet the world of beholders does agree that the most pleasing sights that exist are produced by nature. Why not then capture some of that beauty for your own enjoyment as well as your comfort?

I feel that the innate beauty makes up for some of our lack of creativity and expertise. Nature's own lines and curves in a piece of wood can help you design the piece you need. Many times I have not found wood to correspond to my ideas and I was forced to use what I had. The finished product possessed a charm and singularity that I had not envisioned. After a while, I would not want to trade the piece for my previous design.

You need not be locked into exotic woods and shapes. Ordinary slabs, slices, and cross-sectional cuts make very beautiful furniture.

One of my favorite tables came from a board that another furniture maker threw out because it was cracked. Another time someone gave me a walnut log 5 feet long and 3 feet in diameter to use for firewood. It was rotted in the middle and "useless" to him. Cross-sectional slices were worked up into some of the most interesting tables I have ever made. Nature will offer you more suggestions than you can use. For instance, while I was working on a few pieces of the rotted walnut, I left the other slices outside. By the time I got to them, weeds were growing out of the rotted section. After working up the next table, I dug out all the rot, put a piece of plywood on the bottom of the hole, sealed the cavity with polyurethane, mixed the rotted wood with top soil, threw it back into the hole, and stuck in a geranium. I had a built-in planter.

For that hour or so of work, I received so many compliments that you might have thought I was the Frank Lloyd Wright of the furniture world. Ideas are right there in the wood; just look for them. This is not as difficult as it might seem. If you look at a piece of wood long enough, things will jump out at you. See Figs. I-1 and I-2.

Be patient. Nature is an excellent teacher.

Chapter 1

Overview

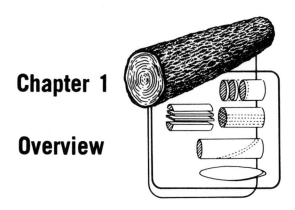

In the days of the early American pioneers, primary concerns were not only pushing West and carving new settlements out of the wilderness, but something even more basic—survival. It boggles the modern mind to imagine the myriad of tasks that filled their daily work day. They had to do everything from building cabins—complete with fireplace for heat and cooking—to growing their own crops and hunting game. All this was done, of course, without the aid of power tools or chain saws. No doubt each day had more demands than they had time for.

Needless to say, they did not devote precious time to interior decorating or furniture design. Cabin furniture was functional and almost always fashioned from rough-cut lumber from trees felled to clear land for a cabin site and farming. Tables, chairs, and cabinets were the main necessities in the early American log cabin.

Being plain and functional does not in any way connote that they were unattractive. Their design of multipurpose furniture is the inspiration of many modern and popular designs. Most of their pieces combined a storage area with a work top. Today we have hutches, enclosed end tables, and coffee tables. We can thank the pioneers for such beautiful pieces.

COLONIAL

As the colonies developed, people settled down to a bit more "modern" living. Land had been cleared, farms were working, industry was developing. People had time to think about more than just surviving. One result was attention to more intricate design and decorating.

1

In the 1700s, the American colonists were incorporating more and more beautiful European furniture designs and decorating ideas. This was hastened by the influx of craftsmen emigrating to the new land. The Chippendale and Queen Ann designs became part of American Colonial life. Having lots of drawers and storage space, these styles adapted the more ornate with the functional. Hard woods were used because they captured the natural beauty through a highly polished finish. The Colonial period turned 180 degrees from painfully plain to highly decorative detail.

SHAKER

In the late eighteenth century, while affluent America was basking in its comfort, there was a small sect of religious fundamentalists called Shakers, was formed. Their uncomplicated way of life dictated their design of furniture.

Simplicity was a feature of their furniture. Function alone controlled design. Style was colored by theological respect and appreciation of God mirrored in nature. Although the design was plain, it had a simplistic attractiveness. The natural beauty of the wood received careful attention. Their craftsmanship was superb. The result has been a legacy of furniture design that blends well in the twentieth-century home or stands in its own right after more than 200 years even though the sect now has few members.

The furniture in this book probably more closely resembles the Shaker style than any other period within the whole gamet of Early American furniture. The bottom line might be a combination of "pioneer" and Shaker. The "free edge" idea comes more from the pioneer style. The square lines and delicate finish of the wood come from the Shaker designs. I feel it is a beautiful marriage of the two periods and I see no end to the popularity of the furniture created in this style.

TOOLS

Saws. You will need a radial arm circular saw or table saw, although a Skil saw will suffice if you are careful. A sabre saw (hand or electric) is also useful.

Drill. Use ⅜″ or ½″ reversible and variable speed drills. Any electric drill will suffice, but use a variable-speed drill for driving screws. Obtain bits of various sizes.

Belt Sander. Hand sanding is possible but it is time-consuming and tiring. A vibrator sander is good, but it is not necessary equipment.

Clamps. Several C-clamps and a couple of furniture clamps made from pipe and ends purchased in any hardware store will be useful.

Miscellaneous. Obtain small tools including a hammer, screwdriver, hand saw, chisel, T-square, level, and carpenters' ruler.

Chapter 2

Choosing Wood

Wood is classified in two main categories. *Hardwood* is from any tree that has a broad leaf. *Softwood* is from any needle-bearing tree or a tree that has scale-like leaves such as conifers.

This does not mean that the wood from these trees is correspondingly hard or soft. Because of this, I will refer to the density of the wood. A less dense wood is softer, lighter, easier to cut and sand. Examples are pine, gumwood, poplar, and white cedar. Common, dense woods that are harder, heavier, more difficult to cut and sand are oak, maple, cherry, and ash.

It is important to know the difference. You don't want to waste your time trying to make a strong frame for a couch by using elm. It has a low tolerance for stress. It is used, however, in cheap commercial furniture. Why put in the time, effort, and money working up what you hope will be a fine piece of furniture when the type of wood will greatly limit its beauty. I will mention here only a few woods in this category (and some readers will disagree with me). These woods are elm, Phillipine mahogany, and willow.

A friend once asked me how to secure the legs to an end table he was making. I stopped at his house one evening to show him how to dowel the legs, and I gasped at what he had worked up. His table was a 4-inch thick diagonal cut from a 15-inch sumac tree. He was very proud of the job he had done; if he had used better wood, his table would have been beautiful. I never told him what wood he had used, but I did suggest that he thoroughly seal the sides, top, and bottom with varnish to prevent the wood from cracking. My real reason was that sumac is a skin irritant to many people and I, for one, am very allergic to it. I feel that sumac is one of nature's poorer productions. It's not even good for firewood.

What wood you use will depend on your taste as well as what is available in your price range or to your chain saw. Choose a wood that is strong enough to take the stress that will be put on it, and it should be interesting enough to have a finish that suits your taste and is worth your efforts.

It is not necessary to become an expert on all woods. There are entirely too many to study. If you find a piece that looks interesting and is not commonly used, work up a small section or scrap piece. If it looks good to *you,* take a whack at it.

WHERE TO FIND WOOD

There are a number of practical advantages for amateur furniture makers who are considering using free-form designs. Sawmills almost always have hard and soft wood in free-form cut. It is a bit more expensive than finding your own, but unless the particular mill is a "rip off" (no pun intended), the piece will not usually be too expensive. My first suggestion is that you check where building lots are being cleared or roads and power lines are being cut through. Often wood will be yours for the asking. This is especially true if you offer a slight remuneration to the foreman.

Many times there is good cherry, oak, ash, maple or pine being taken down. All of these woods make beautiful furniture. I have also helped my neighbors and friends cut down trees that had to be removed. In that way, I have acquired some very interesting pieces of wood at no expense.

WOOD CHARACTERISTICS

White Ash. From Central and Eastern United States. White to light brown, prominent grain with distinct elliptical rings, hard, strong, rather difficult to work, warps and checks some. Used widely in furniture as frames requiring strength and in the exposed parts of mainly bedroom furniture. Stains well and resembles oak.

Beech. From Central and Eastern North America. Slightly reddish or white, grain not very prominent. Strong, hard, warps and shrinks a lot. Has a tendency to dry rot, moderately hard to work, but finishes well. Used for furniture frames requiring strength. Also for exposed areas of furniture because of its quality for polishing. It is found mostly in country-style furniture.

Birch. Found in any temperature zone. Of the many varieties of birch, the yellow is important. The heartwood (center) is light to dark reddish-brown, the sapwood (outer part) is white and the irregular grain is not very distinctive. It is hard and heavy, does not shrink nor warp much, is not too difficult to work and finishes to a beautiful, well-polished, interesting piece, if the heartwood and sapwood are left intact. Used in furniture either for structural strength or exterior natural finish. This wood can be stained to imitate walnut or mahogany.

Cedar. Found in North Pacific Coast and in mountains of North America. Reddish-brown to white and is very close grained. It is surprisingly soft wood, weak, and light weight. With this characteristic it is easily worked. It shrinks little and resists decay. Good for outdoor projects. Red cedar resists decay. Good for outdoor projects. Red cedar resists moths. Mostly used for outdoor furniture, fences and siding.

Cherry. Found throughout the United States. It is light to dark reddish-brown. The younger trees have a lighter sapwood giving the two-toned effect of walnut or birch. It is close-grained, strong, durable and moderately hard. Because it polishes well it is used in Colonial and Early American styles of furniture.

Cypress. A southern wood. Shades vary from slightly reddish to almost black. It weathers to a gray, if exposed. It is moderately strong, light in weight, and resists decay. It is used mostly outdoors for furniture, porches, decks and siding.

Elm. Found throughout the United States. It is light gray with brown and red streaks. Sapwood is whitish. It is a heavy wood but not very strong. It has an open, porous grain that is hard to work. This wood shrinks and swells quite a bit. Used sparingly in furniture. Nevertheless, thick crosscut slices do make impressive tables.

Fir. Found in the Pacific coast area. It varies from yellowish, reddish, or brownish and is a soft wood yet rather strong. It tends to split and check profusely and does not finish well. It is used widely for the structural parts of cheap furniture.

Gum. Found in Eastern United States. It is a reddish-brown and often has very interesting pigment streaks. It is relatively hard and strong, but will warp, shrink, swell and rot. It is, however, easy to work and finishes well. Used for both interior and exterior parts of indoor furniture.

Mahogany. From Central and South America and Africa. The heartwood is a pale to deep reddish-brown with an interesting interwoven grain that gives it a high value. It is medium hard and strong, bends and shrinks little, but it is easy to work. The finish takes a high polish and makes beautiful furniture in natural finish as well as bleached or stained. It is an expensive wood because it is imported and much in demand. Philippine mahogany is a less expensive imitation that does not have the grain characteristics or the finish capabilities. The variety from the Philippines shrinks and warps more, is softer, and less durable. This variety is used almost exclusively in paneling and to mimic the American and African variety. It is a poor substitute.

Maple. From Central and Eastern United States. Whitish to tan in color, close straight grain or birds' eye. It is hard, heavy, strong and swells and shrinks little. It is hard to work, but it takes a good finish and it polishes very well. It is often used for furniture and flooring.

Oak. Generally, you will see white or red oak from the temperate zones. The white goes from pale to light brown. Red oak has reddish tint. Both have a straight, open grain. They are hard, strong and work well. Used in furniture and flooring.

Pine. All varieties are similar in characteristics. It is found in all temperate zones. Found in white through reddish-brown. It is a close grained soft wood, and is not strong. It warps, swells, shrinks, bends and does all kinds of tricks when drying. It works well and takes a good finish with or without stain. Used for furniture, paneling and structural studding.

Poplar. From Eastern United States. White to light brown. A soft, weak, lightweight wood that is very easy to work. Finishes and stains well. Used in inexpensive furniture. A type of poplar, commonly called Tulip Poplar, has splashes of purple grain through it and makes inexpensive and yet interesting furniture and cabinets.

Redwood. Found in Pacific Coast, United States. Reddish-brown wood lightens in the sun and becomes gray if weathered. Has parallel grain and a wild unruly grain in the burls. It is hard, durable and finishes to a high polish. Used in more expensive furniture and outdoor furniture, fences, and siding. The burls are fascinating in sliced form and they are used for wall clocks and hangings.

Rosewood. Imported from India and Brazil. Light to deep reddish-brown. Grain has irregular streaks and swirls of black or deep brown. It is hard, strong and durable. It is becoming very popular today for furniture because of its deep, rich tones and ability to take a high polish. To stain this wood is foolish.

Teak. From parts of Asia. It is a straight-grained, yellowish to pale brownish and has a grain of narrow stripes. This wood is extremely hard and durable. It works well and is usually given an oil finish. It is used for carved furniture and boat decks.

Tupelo Gum. From Southeastern United States. It is a brownish-gray with a white sapwood. It is somewhat softer than sweetgum, but it has the same use.

Walnut (American or Black). This most popular furniture wood is found in the Central and Eastern United States. It is light to dark chocolate brown. It might have dark, irregular blotches or streaks, varied tones of swirls, or dark and distinctively outlined figures. It is hard, heavy, strong, fairly easy to work, and it takes a beautiful finish. It might warp some and split if not cured with care. It is used in expensive furniture and paneling.

Walnut (English). This walnut is fawn-color with dark swirls and figures. Imported for American furniture.

Chapter 3

Seasoned Timber

A piece of wood is considered seasoned when it contains no more than 20 to 22 percent of the moisture content of the live tree. Removing most of the moisture is imperative because the wood will "move" while it is drying. In other words it will shrink, warp, or crack.

There are many ways to dry wood. The quickest way is kiln drying. This takes only a month or two, but it is expensive. Another way is to dry it naturally. Allow the boards to stand *on end* and off the ground. Put 2 × 4s between them and the ground so that your board will not draw the moisture from the ground. Standing the board up allows the moisture and sap to run with the grain and the wood will dry faster than if you lay it down. Do not let the upright boards press against one another. This will cut off the flow of air around the board and allow moisture to remain in that spot. It will allow mildew to form and it might even result in rotted wood.

The air space that you have between the boards need not be more than 1 inch, but some air around the entire board is a must. Never allow direct sunlight to hit the wood. This causes uneven drying and results in warping and splitting. Some prefer to coat the ends of each board with a liberal coat of hot wax or paraffin to prevent the ends of the board from drying more quickly than the center. It will slow the drying process slightly, but it is worth it.

Others prefer to coat the entire board with a commercial wood preservative. This does not change the color or tone of the wood, but it does slow the drying process to help prevent cracking. If your wood is interesting or important enough to you, then the added effort of treating it with preservative and wax and the wait necessary to cure it will be well worthwhile.

A rule of thumb is that for each inch of thickness it takes one year of drying time. For example, if your board is 2 inches thick, it should dry for two years. It is true that some woods dry more quickly, but you can never be sure unless you have it moisture-tested at a mill or lumber yard that has the proper meter.

Even after it is dry, there is no guarantee that when the finished product is brought into different temperature and humidity conditions that it will not move. That is one reason for securing each board with glue and plenty of screws. That should hold it in place for you.

Chapter 4

Coffee Table

A coffee table or small utility table is a good place to start if you have never made furniture. It will give you a feel for the free-form style. It is less work than the larger couch and chair projects and it will allow you to quickly see your results. Because most do-it-yourselfers cannot work constantly on a project, you might tend to become frustrated or lose interest unless there is some motivation to stay with it. The noticeable progress with each few hours' work on a small project might provide you with the incentive to keep on going. For a first project, I suggest building a small table.

Your purpose for making a table will determine the shape and type of wood you select. If you want to make something just to get a feel for this type of activity, you will still probably have some idea in mind as to what you will do with the finished piece. This is fine, but it limits your choice of wood. If the only available spot in your den for a table is in the corner, you won't select a 6-foot slab to work on. Do not select a piece that you really don't care for just because it is available and you want to make something. Working on something that you feel is unimportant will be boring and you might lose interest. It would be better to wait for the right piece.

The piece you select can be slab from a log, a cross-section, a diagonal cut lengthwise along a log, or any other possible cut you can conceive. See Fig. 4-1. Often the center slab is used for a coffee table and the slab next to it, which will be a bit narrower, is cut in half and used for two end tables.

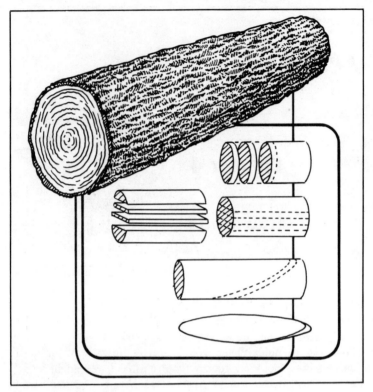

Fig. 4-1. Various types of cuts from a log.

Once I saw a cross-section slice of an oak tree, about 3 feet diameter, used as a round coffee table and the next slice was cut in half and each half used as an end table. See Fig. 4-2. This was very impressive. My preference is an irregular-shaped piece of walnut with some deep tone grain figures and a few small rotten spots or holes. To me this has personality.

Round tables from cross-section cuts of the tree are also impressive if the wood has a noticeable grain or if the grain can be accentuated in some way as in stained ash. I have seen beautiful tables like this made of walnut, ash, pine, cherry, cottonwood, redwood, and even elm.

Here are some suggestions that might add a touch more personality to your table. If you slab a log and the slab you want is not determined by a specific width, take it from a section with a branch or two coming out. Then cut the branch off. This usually gives a slight flow of grain outside of the table and breaks up the side with

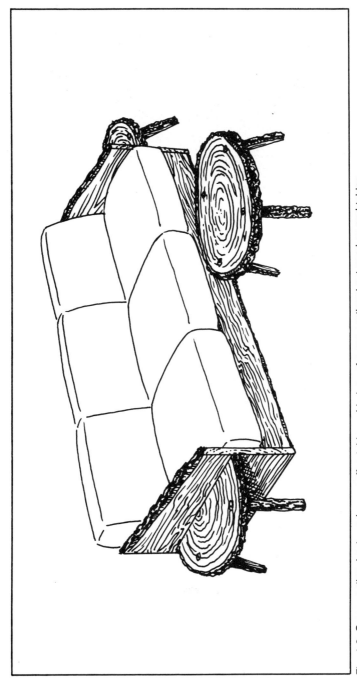

Fig. 4-2. Cross-sectional cut used as a coffee table and halves of cross-sectional cut used as end tables.

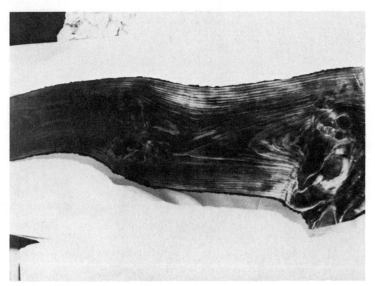

Fig. 4-3. This pine coffee table demonstrates the flow of the grain that was cut off the wide side.

an area of grain from the branch. You do not necessarily have to cut the branch off square. It might follow the curve of the side of the table or go opposite to it (Fig. 4-3). Remember, there are not too many right angles in nature.

For all of these tables you can leave the bark on or remove it. See Figs. 4-4 and 4-5. This is mainly a matter of taste or what other pieces you want to mix the table with. My taste is to stay with the bark as much as possible in order to preserve the naturalness.

Fig. 4-4. The bark on the table (both top and legs).

Fig. 4-5. A walnut end table. The legs have the bark removed. The base of the lamp is a wedge cut of walnut also with the bark intact.

15

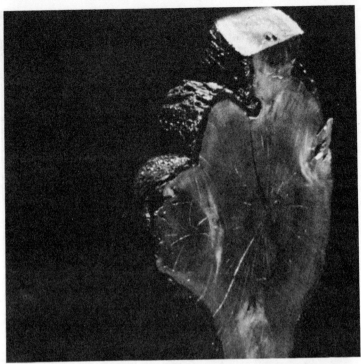

Fig. 4-6. The bark is intact on a cross section of cherry that is irregular in shape.

If the bark is peeling off, as it sometimes will, carefully take all the loose bark and glue it back in place tightly with finishing brads long enough to get a good bite into the wood. Place these nails in the crevasse of the bark and hammer them flush with an awl. A large nail is not recommended; it might slip off and chip the bark. Wipe off all the glue that oozes out *while it is wet.*

Allow the glue to dry the recommended time before sanding or finishing the piece. Be sure to put the bark back in the exact spot from where you removed it.

Before you glue, remove any sand or dirt from both surfaces. Quite often there will be worms or bugs living between the bark and the sapwood. Each species of bug does its own thing, but usually there are little tunnels of a powder that, unless it is thoroughly cleaned out, will prevent a good bond for the glue.

Bark is especially impressive on a cross-sectional cut. The slice is most impressive if it is irregular in shape rather than perfectly round. The more the bark dips in toward the heartwood, the more interesting the piece becomes. See Fig. 4-6.

If you are fortunate enough to find a piece where two trees have grown together or where the cut was made at the junction of the trunk going into two large branches, the piece will have two cores. These pieces make very impressive tables. I once saw a piece cut from where a walnut and a cherry tree had grown together. There was no definite line of demarcation between the two woods; one flowed into the other. This is so rare that the unfinished boards were priced in the thousands.

Chapter 5

Legs

The legs for a piece of furniture should enhance the piece by carrying through the theme and lines of the top while not distracting from it. They can be distinct but they should not draw your primary attention. In general, the wood for the legs is the same as that of the top or the complete piece (but it need not be). If you take your main slab from a fallen tree or large branch, there will likely be other branches available that, upon investigation, might be usable. Branches that go into a Y or crooked branches tend to get away from the standard look. This is advisable if the table top is not unusual. See Fig. 5-1.

If you have acquired a really unusual piece, branches might not be available. If you can acquire the same wood for use as legs, it is usually a good idea to go with "sameness." But you need not be married to that technique. You can mix woods in the same piece. As a matter of fact, if you have a very unusual tabletop, such as a slice of redwood root or the root cut of birds'-eye maple, you probably are better off with very plain legs. You certainly could mix the redwood with cherry legs and the maple with birch or oak legs and not lose the continuity or distract from the top. A general rule might be that the more "busy" the top, the plainer the legs.

There are a number of tricks you can use to spice up the legs. If the tabletop juts out in any way, you could place the leg at that area and get away from the standard positioning of the legs in the perfect rectangle form. See Fig. 5-2.

If the table is narrow at one end, use three legs on it. Have two at the wide end and one at the narrow end. You will have to trade a bit of stability of the table for this. If the wide end has enough space between the legs, it should be sturdy enough. Stability can be gained by making the legs shorter and the table lower.

Some people like to put the tabletop on a base of driftwood. This is a matter of preference. Be careful that your base is not too busy or it will detract from the top. I prefer to put a glass top on an interesting driftwood base.

You could be able to take a cue from the type of furniture you are mixing. If you are mixing your home-built furniture with period furniture you might find that copying the legs of the existing furniture will fit well on your piece. For example, an Early American style can be matched with heavy square legs. See Fig. 5-1. These can also be notched to pick up the Early American flavor.

Notches are easy if you have a belt sander. Don't use the flat part of the sander. Use the part of the wheel in the front and sand the groove to the depth you like. Try not to be symmetrical with these grooves. Make them different depths and lengths.

All legs need not be rounded or four-sided. They could be three-sided or five-sided, or have bark on one side or one-half side. They could taper or be of uniform width. They might have knots or

Fig. 5-1. A Y-shaped leg on one end of an 8' oak coffee table. The cut on this table is diagonal.

19

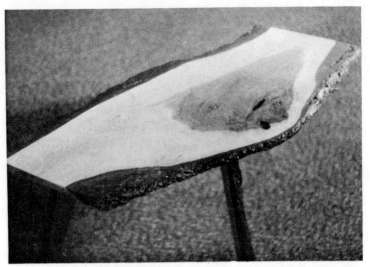

Fig. 5-2. A three-legged utility table. The middle leg is at the widest part of the table.

protrusions where branches were cut off. If the leg bends, it would be a good idea to take a slice off the bend. This will expose the inner grain. See Fig. 5-4.

You might want a pedestal-type support from a piece of log. This is acceptable, but it will give a much heavier look to the table. I use this idea for garden furniture more than for den pieces or living-room pieces. See Fig. 5-5. Use your imagination. If you have a choice of logs, cut one where the branches come out (so that you have protrusions at ground level). Or cut a piece with branches on it and cut them off so you break up the plain pattern. Or have the branches come out toward the top as arm supports.

Don't be afraid to take a chance on an unusual wood. If you see an interesting branch, grab it, cut it to size, and hold it under your table. If it doesn't match, there is no problem. But you might be pleasantly surprised.

When attaching the legs to the tabletop, there are two primary things to keep in mind:

■ You want the table strong so that someone leaning on it will not break the legs off.

■ You want it steady so that it will not wobble on uneven logs. Both of these things can be obtained with a little planning and care.

There are a number of ways to attach legs. Some are rather easy and some require more work. Depending on the position of the leg and the height of the tabletop, the top of the leg might be totally out of sight and you could drill through the leg into the top. Or you could screw a piece of ½" plywood to the top of the leg and leave it about ⅝" over on each side. Then screw through the plywood into the tabletop. This, plus glue, will make it very steady.

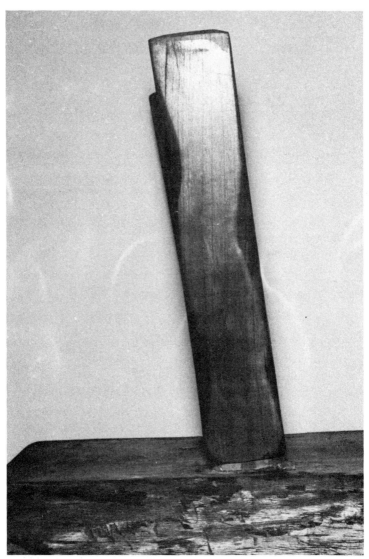

Fig. 5-3. Note the notches sanded into the legs of this cherry coffee table to better blend with an Early American decor.

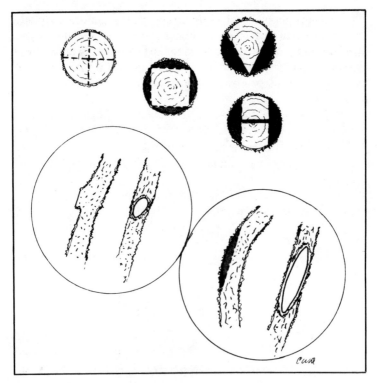

Fig. 5-4. A few ways legs can be cut from branches.

My choice is to use a single dowel for each leg. If the table legs are at least 2 inches square in diameter, you can use a ⅝″ dowel. Don't use a dowel that is too thin because you sacrifice strength. I never use a dowel of less than ½″ diameter. This allows me, at all times, a good ¾″ of leg all around the dowel. With heavier legs, 2½″ or 3″ in diameter, use ¾″ dowel.

Insert the dowel about 1½″ into the leg and about the same into the table if your top is thick enough. If your top is only an inch thick, go ¾″ deep.

When you drill the hole for the dowel, use the same size bit as you have dowel (½″ bit for a ½″ dowel). If you are using commercial dowels, they do come with a spiral groove carved in them and are ready to use. If you make your own dowels, you must cut in some kind of an escape route for the glue when you hammer in the dowel. If the glue is trapped under the dowel, as you hammer it the dowel will act as a hydraulic piston and split the leg or maybe even your table top.

You have several choices for turning your round piece of wood into a usable dowel. The easiest way is to run a belt sander or a hand plane down the whole length of the ½" round (or whatever size you are using) and flatten one side of it before you cut it to size. Or you can drag the round across a hand saw and dig grooves on all sides of the round.

Drill the legs and the table. Keep the drill straight. If you want to go only an inch or so deep, put a piece of masking tape around the drill bit at the desired distance from the tip. This will show you where to stop drilling. Cut the dowel to size; this means a hair shorter than the combined depth of both holes. Round the edges of the dowel. Remember the bit is sort of round so you have to work off the edges so the dowel will fit.

Apply a wood glue to the dowel and in the holes; follow directions on the glue bottle. You may have to let the glue set for a few minutes. Hammer the dowel into either the leg or the table first. Position the leg and hammer it home. Make sure it is tight and straight. Wipe off all excess glue. Even a small smudge will show up through stain or varnish. Let it dry according to the manufacturers' recommended time.

When the legs are dry, turn the table over. If you cut the legs evenly and fastened them tightly, the table should be level and steady. If it is not steady, place the table on a level surface, shim up the legs with a *small* piece (or pieces) of wood or cardboard until it is steady and level. Now measure from whatever level surface you used, let's say a floor without a rug, to the bottom of one, two, or even three legs that are shimmed up.

Fig. 5-5. A rough-cut cross section of cherry on a pedestal base. This was used as a utility table in a wooded backyard near a barbecue pit.

Fig. 5-6. End table legs with a small section of the bark left on. This table is cherry.

The measurement of the leg that is fartherest off the floor is now your magic number and that is the leg that you *do not* cut. Suppose the shortest leg is ½″ off the floor. Measure *from the floor*, ½″ on the other legs and mark them. The amount you cut off each leg might be different, but if your mark is exactly ½″ from the floor your table will be level and steady.

If you use only three legs, as you might on a round utility table, no matter how uneven they are the table will not wobble. You need only to make sure that the table is level. Use the same method as above to level it.

Another method of leveling a table is to lay it upside down on a smooth, level floor. Take another end table or coffee table the same height as you want your new one. Push it against the legs at one end. Mark them by using the top of the table as a guide. Do the same to the other end. This is easy if all four legs are above the top of your "guideline" table. But if one is shorter, measure the distance of the shortest to the top of your guideline. Let's assume it is ⅜″ short. Move the lines on the other legs down ⅜″. It will come out even. You can do this even if two or more legs are short. Measure the ⅜″ down and mark the legs.

Fig. 5-7. A walnut coffee table with legs in a triangle configuration and the bark completely on one side.

If you are careful in marking and cutting, your table will not wobble and it will be level. When you put something on it, the item won't slide down the table to the person sitting next to you.

Chapter 6

Sofa

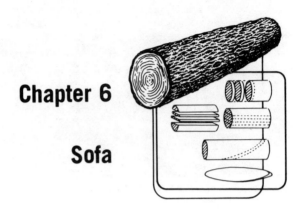

Depending on your purpose in making furniture, you might want to take as many shortcuts as possible—saving time and money—or you might want to start from zero and build everything from the ground up. Perhaps you would even want to go all out and use only doweled and mitered joints. A piece of furniture—where you have fashioned each slab and joint and you can boast of having used no hardware—is something in which you certainly can have pride. Some people like to work that way. On the other hand, if it looks good and is sturdy it is also worthwhile. You can glue, tie, screw, and bolt the insides of a sofa or chair and have the outside look clean, smooth, and classy.

This chapter offers a few hints on how to take shortcuts by using a ready-made frame. I emphasize the value of saving time and money as well as lessening the demand on your experience and ability. I have found it very satisfactory to take an old living-room set and reuse the ready-made frame. This technique affords you the opportunity to bypass the work and the money involved in building a frame from scratch. With this method, you have a starting point that is probably square, level, and sturdy.

CHOOSING A FRAME

When I look for an old couch, I look for one that has straight lines and the size I need. I do not look on the city dump. I have been successful in getting couches from friends of friends of friends who are either getting new living room furniture or throwing away a sofa from a den or recreation room. They are usually grateful to have someone haul it away. All my friends know that I am always looking for old furniture and they tell me when some pops up. Before I had a pickup truck, I had to tie the sofa on the roof of the car and jam a chair into the trunk. If you really need it, you will find a way to get it. I have never paid for a frame yet.

To determine whether the frame is worth using, first strip all the fabric and padding from the couch. Leaving only the frame, springs, webbing, or whatever is used for a seat. Once you have stripped the couch, you can take a good look at it in order to determine whether it is suitable for use. The following are features that would warrant you rejecting it.

■ Sides that are badly bowed and cannot be easily removed.

■ A front board that is badly bowed. Tack a string to one end of the front board and pull it tight along the front edge. This will give you a straight line from which to judge.

■ A very ornate or high back that cannot be readily squared off.

■ The back and kickboard having been finished in relief that cannot be easily removed.

■ The whole frame being out of square more than 1 inch.

■ Main braces broken that are not easily repairable.

■ Any main spar—the boards running lengthwise along the couch—that are broken.

■ Springs that are popping out in all directions and cannot easily be retied.

■ Webbing or hemp that is rotted or sagging. If your frame has this sort of seat, you might be able to replace it with a piece of plywood.

■ Wood that is rotted or badly split.

You will have to decide whether your frame is fit to rework or to repair easily. If it would involve too much work, it might be easier to look around for another couch frame or to build your own frame rather than get involved in the work of fixing the one you have. But don't take lightly the idea of redoing an old couch as opposed to building your own. A point to consider is that old furniture is very often of high quality workmanship and good hardwood. Some of the frames I have used are of better wood than I could afford to buy. Some have more sophisticated workmanship than I have time to produce. Some come complete with springs that are expensive and look more complicated to install than I care to duplicate. Besides, springs are more comfortable than any type of seat that I would build.

PREPARING THE FRAME

When you have selected a couch, stripped, inspected, and accepted it for use, prepare it as follows:

■ Remove or at least hammer flush all loose nails and staples.

■ Reglue any loose joints and strengthen them with screws if necessary.

■ Tie any loose springs. Use any knot that will hold.

■ If it looks soiled or dirty, you should wipe it down with a strong detergent and then give it a liberal going over with a can of spray disinfectant.

REMOVING THE ARMS

Because your finished free-form piece will probably include sides and a kickboard, you will most likely want to remove the existing sides of your old piece. Study the construction of the frame before you start cutting pieces off or you will wind up with a pile of wood and springs that resemble a couch only in your memory.

Often the sides are the sole support of the seat frame and the back frame. These might not be attached to one another in any way. If this is the case, remove only the arm section and not the whole side.

In Fig. 6-1, the unshaded side is the original frame stripped to the springs. It has no cushion on the seat. The shaded area is what it will look like when the arm has been removed. If the whole frame is supported and the sides are attached to that support, you might be able to remove the complete side without affecting the supporting structure. Do whatever is easier. You must take at least the arm off because you don't want the old sides showing. You want only the free-form side visible. See Fig. 6-1.

PLANNING

Now that you have the frame clean and the arms or sides off, you are in a better position to plan some of the details of your creation. First consider how far off the floor you want your free-form edge to be. This depends on your taste and at least one practical point. I have made furniture that used the kickboard and sides as legs with a couple of pieces of short 2 × 4s as legs in the back.

The couch actually sits on the floor. This, however, is hard on the rug. It is great in a large colonial-style room with exposed random-plank flooring. If the sofa is to be used on a rug, I prefer to

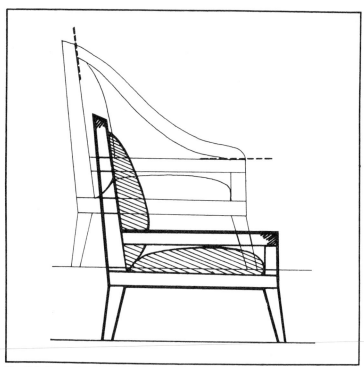

Fig. 6-1. Removing arms of old frame. The unshaded side is the original frame stripped of upholstery. The shaded side is what it will look like when the arms have been removed. The dotted line shows the places of the cut.

Fig. 6-2. The distance of the kickboard off the floor.

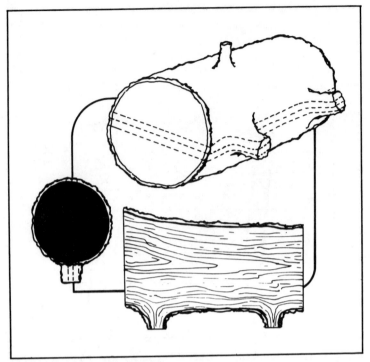

Fig. 6-3. The side of the couch that incorporates the free-form edge into legs.

run the free-form edge as close as possible to the floor. The weight of the piece rests on the six legs. Putting coasters under the legs saves the rug and the piece still has the effect of flowing into the floor. See Fig. 6-2.

You are also free to make the kickboard an inch or so more narrow and have a bit of the legs showing. If you make the legs longer to accomplish this, you must be careful not to have the top of the cushion any more than 16″ or at the most 17″ from the floor.

If you do not intend to use the legs that are already on the frame, you might be lucky enough to have found a slab of free-form with knobs or limbs that would make natural legs. See Fig. 6-3.

Next consider how you want your kickboard to fit into the sides. Do you want it to butt against the side as in A of Fig. 6-4 or be notched into it as in B of Fig. 6-4? Would you prefer the side to be completely notched out to admit the kickboard? It would extend to the outside extremities of the couch as in C of Figure 6-4.

The decision must be made before you can determine the length of your kickboard. I will describe first the butt joint (A) as

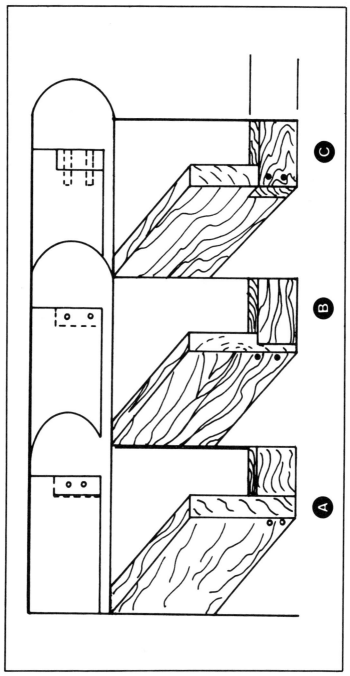

Fig. 6-4. The kickboard attached to the free form side by: (A) butt joint; (B) rabbet joint; and (C) notched joint.

shown in Fig. 6-4. It is the easiest. Near the end of the chapter, I will mention joints B and C in case you prefer these.

DETERMINING THE SQUARE

Your next step is the most important if you want a couch that is square at the corners and does not look like a developing trapezoid. Place a large T-square with the short side against the front (where your kickboard will be attached) and the long side against the existing side of the couch frame. Keep the short side tight against the front and let the long arm touch the side. If the arms of the square lie flat and tight against the front and the side (on both ends of your frame), you are lucky and all corners are square. See A of Fig. 6-5.

But if you find that your T-square is flat and tight against the front portion and touches the side only at one point—such as the center or the back—you can be sure that the old frame has given in to stress over the years and the sides have bowed or are at least out of square. This is not uncommon and need not cause a problem.

MEASURING THE KICKBOARD

Hold the short end of your T-square on the existing front board

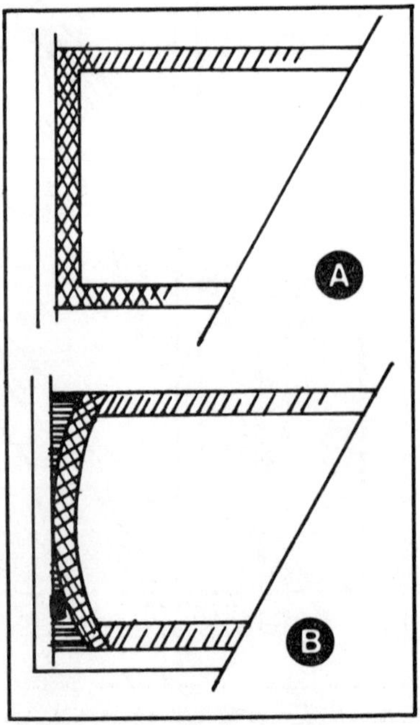

Fig. 6-5. The use of the T-square to check the angles of the frame and the degree of warp in the sides.

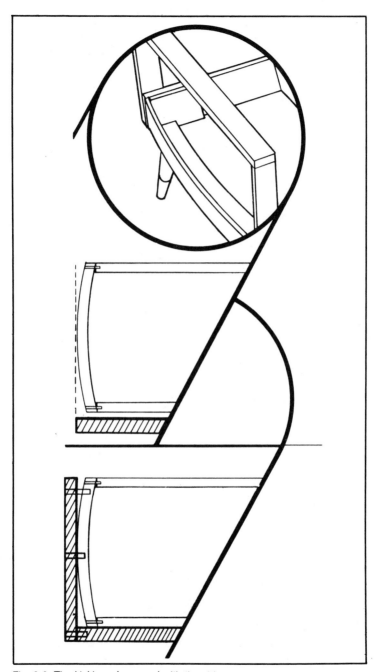

Fig. 6-6. The kickboard squared with the side.

of your frame and, allowing the long side of the T-square to touch the warped side of the couch, you will get a 90-degree angle for the side regardless of the curve of the old frame. Where the long side of your T-square is at this time is exactly where your free-form side will be. If your kickboard extends to the inside line of the long arm of your T-square, the kickboard will be in position for the front of your new side to be attached. The point where the T-square touches the frame side will be the second point of contact for your new side. This will make your side perfectly square with the front and that side will be exactly where the T-square was. See Fig. 6-5.

Now for the actual measurement. With the T-square in place, measure from the *inside* of the long arm 6″ and mark the distance on the front board of the couch. Do the same at the other end and mark it. Then measure the distance between your marks and add the 6 inches from each end, or 1 foot, and you have the needed length of your kickboard. Assuming this length is 91″, and the actual length of your front frame is 90″, this extra inch will insure that your sides are square. See Fig. 6-6.

If the sides of your frame were perfectly square to start with, then measure the existing front of the frame (the whole frame, end to end). This will be exactly the length of your kickboard. If it is, for example, 90″, it will be a long couch that is functional in seating four people or in having one tall person stretch out comfortably.

CONSTRUCTION OF THE KICKBOARD

You might want the free edge of the kickboard to remain on both the top and the bottom. You are free to do so provided that these edges are somewhat straight. If you use a kickboard with a double free edge, I suggest that you use a butt joint rather than notch it. This way you need only square the ends to the proper length and you are in business. But if your kickboard is wide enough, it is advisable in many cases to square the top edge the cushions will sit on and leave the free edge only across the bottom. See Fig. 6-7.

I rarely find a slab straight enough to use as is. It is usually necessary to square the top in order to insure comfort and equal dimension at each end (Fig. 6-7). Make the top of your new board flush with the top of the existing frame. Do not have it extend below the existing legs. This will insure the proper height of the seat. Keep in mind, before you cut anything off, that you must leave the board wide enough to reach the floor or whatever distance off the floor that you decided.

Note that the thickness of your kickboard will lengthen the

width of the seat or cushion area the same amount. This is not a problem if you are making new cushions. You can make them fit what you have. If you are using old cushions, you should make the new board as thin as possible—no more than 1″. No matter which way you do, do not make this board too thick. The seat would then become inordinately wide and uncomfortable. If you are making new cushions, I would confine the width of the kickboard to no more than 2″ (no matter how thick you make your side pieces).

Measure from the top of the frame (to which you will attach your kickboard) to the floor. I assume that you have 12″. If you want this facing board to touch the floor, then make the board 12″. If you want it to be an inch off the floor, make the board 11″ wide. If you are dealing with one solid board rather than two or three pieces for your kickboard, then draw your line the 11″ or 12″ from the free edge you want to keep.

Make sure your line is even. Check it with a string. Make your

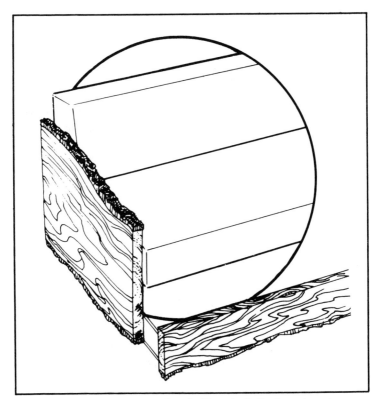

Fig. 6-7. Shows the placement of the kickboard with the top squared.

cut with a hand-held circular saw if you have one. You could use a sabre saw if you are careful and if you go slow. I don't like to use a sabre saw for this type of cutting because the blade tends to follow the line of soft grain instead of your drawn line.

You can always use a handsaw. Go slow and keep the saw at a right angle to your board. It is best that this kickboard be one continuous slab. If this is not possible, you could use two or even three pieces to fabricate it.

If your kickboard is made of pieces, for example two pieces 45" each or three pieces 30" each, try to make the free edge of each piece match or meet (in some way) the piece next to it. This can be done in the planning stage by playing the jigsaw puzzle game. Lay the boards out and position them so that you get a match of the free-form butted ends or at least get them to match as closely as possible. You might be able to turn a board over and reverse the free-form edge. This is provided that the reverse side of your board is finishable and in some way will match the others. Make sure the bevel of the free edge stays uniform.

I would suggest you do this before you cut each board to its preferred width. This will give you the opportunity to match the ends more closely and to get a more free-flowing kickboard.

If you are locked into using the boards in a certain way, because of grain or matching knots or because the bevel will go only one way, you might have to shave off the corner of the free edge in order to make it match the one to which it will be butted. See Fig. 6-8. When you make your cut, attempt to keep the same texture of the existing edges and lean the bevel to the same angle of the board you want to meet.

If you are fortunate enough to have boards with free edges that have a uniform bevel (all in one direction) you have no problem. With some boards, the bevel will roll from one side to the other. In either case, shave or plane off enough to meet the next board. Disturb the natural edge only as far back as necessary and still make the edge "flow." Control the bevel to wind up the same as the next board (as shown in Fig. 6-8).

Be extremely careful to make the end cuts on these pieces so that they will butt with a clean joint. A hint for getting a flush joint on two pieces of wood is to clamp them together at the joint you want to make straight. See Fig. 6-9. With the open edge up, clamp the pieces firmly to a workbench or a table and use buffer boards so that the clamps won't dent the slab. Cut squarely through the joint with a circular saw or handsaw so that you get part of each board. Remove the clamp from one of the boards, butt them tightly again, and reclamp. Repeat the cut.

Do this as often as necessary until you have your last cut taking a sliver off the complete side of each board. They will fit together perfectly. Do this before you cut the length of your kickboard to the 90″ or 91″ that you want because you could lose as much as ½″ in this process.

Again clamp the pieces together on a workbench or a table. Measure and draw a line for the cut across the top. Remove the clamp and cut the boards.

ATTACHING THE KICKBOARD

Unless you intend to change the free-form wood at a later date, or to remove it for upholstering in the future, I suggest you glue all the pieces at the time you screw or dowel the boards in place. This makes for tighter furniture. It is always a good idea to apply the glue over as much of the area as possible. If you are putting a new board onto a full-faced couch front, for example, then glue both surfaces completely.

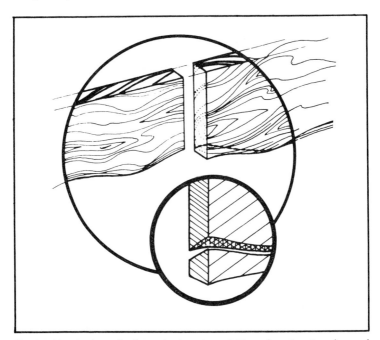

Fig. 6-8. How to shave the free edge to get a matching edge when two pieces of free-form board are butted.

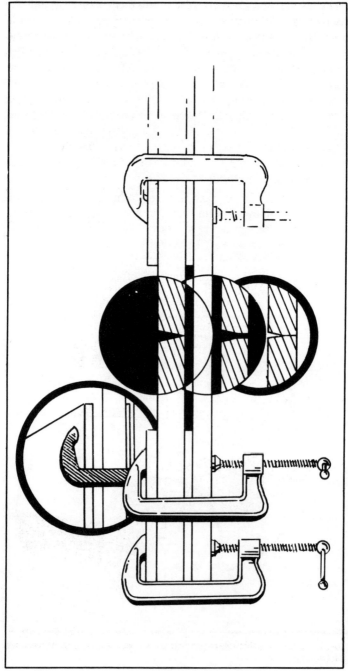

Fig. 6-9. How to clamp and saw the ends to get a clean butt joint.

For best results, a good wood glue should be used; follow the manufacturers' directions carefully. After gluing each piece in place, check the position with a T-square on each side and across the top. Insert all screws or dowels in the holes that you have drilled through the frame. Do this before the glue dries and then also clamp the kickboard with C-clamps as much as necessary.

Fasten with screws, top and bottom, a solid kickboard about every 18″ and a sectioned kickboard at each corner of each piece and about every 14″ between. Make sure all screws are tight and let the glue dry for 24 hours or according to directions on the glue package. Be sure to use a buffer board when you use any clamp. There is no wood hard enough that will not mark or dent under the end of a C-clamp when you pull it up tight.

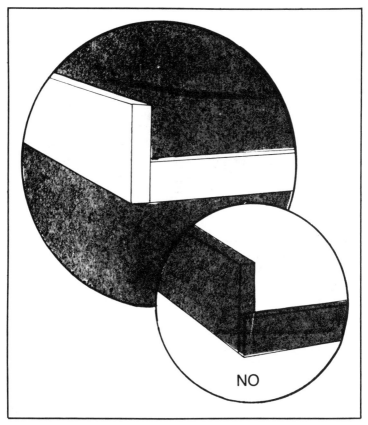

Fig. 6-10. How to fasten the kickboard to acquire a square corner, and how not to fasten it.

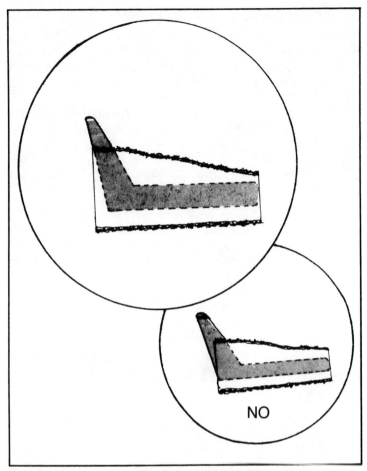

Fig. 6-11. How to measure the proper length of the side pieces.

CONSTRUCTING THE SIDE PIECES

If you have decided to use the butt joint, butt the end of the kickboard against the side free-form piece (as in Fig. 6-10) rather than the end of your side board against the back of the kickboard. You want the sides the same height off the floor as the kickboard. You also want the sides to extend back far enough so that from a side view you will not see the back of the couch extending beyond the side plank. See Fig. 6-11.

Trim the front of the side boards square with the bottom edge. Make sure it is absolutely square. Hold it up to the side of the couch and block the bottom so that it is even with the bottom of the

40

kickboard. Make sure that the bottom of the side is level with the floor. You want to make your mark for the back cut far enough to cover the entire back without having your new board extend beyond the back any further than necessary. The point to mark is the inner section of the top of your free form side with the back of the couch frame. See Fig. 6-11.

Place your side piece flat on the floor again. With the T-square—the short side even with the bottom edge and the long side touching your new mark—draw a line for your back edge. Check that it is parallel with the front cut by measuring the distances along the bottom and the top. A normal couch would have a side of about 33″ (see Fig. 6-12).

If the edges are not parallel and square with the bottom, they will only be a slight bit off and you can remeasure and square them before you make your back cut. Now use this new side as a pattern for the other side of your couch. Mark it. Cut it. Both sides should match.

ATTACHING THE SIDE PIECES

In fastening the sides, use the same principle that you did with the kickboard. Predrill all screw holes through the frame. Glue the seat frame only. Place the side in position and anchor screws through the seat frame only into the side board. Do not, at this point, either glue or put screws through the back frame into the new side. You will need this area open when you upholster the back.

Clamp the side piece to both the seat frame and the back frame and allow it to dry. You could even use angle iron braces on the inside for added support. Be careful that no screws or braces show above the cushion line. Keep in mind also that the cushion will be depressed when someone is sitting on it and the line will be lower.

If by chance both side boards of your sofa do not have a free edge that exactly matches, don't worry. You will not always get symmetrical pieces. Remember that you are using nature's form and that nature is not always symmetrical. Rarely can you get a perfect match unless you get the boards from either side of the center cut of a log. With this type of cut, you do get matching sides for a couch or tables. This is called the "matchbook" effect. See Chapter 19.

The side piece can be notched as in B or C of Fig. 6-4. If you decide to use a B or C joint, you must make this decision before you cut your kickboard to its proper length because these joints will add to that length.

If you intend to use joint C (the easier of the two), you need only to mark the width of the kickboard and the thickness of it on your side pieces. Use the butt end of the kickboard as a template and hold it against your side piece with the front side of your new armpiece already cut square (as shown in A of Fig. 6-4).

Fig. 6-12. This sofa has cherry wood sides and a kickboard. It has an oil rubbed finish. It is upholstered with a rust-colored suede.

Then mark the back and top of the kickboard on the inside of your armpiece. Cut out the complete piece. Use the inside edge of the lines you drew in order to insure a tight fit. I suggest that you use a handsaw for this. The extra length of your kickboard will then be twice the thickness of the side. You can dowel it if you prefer.

The joint shown in B of Fig. 6-4 is measured the same way. And then half the thickness of the side slab is marked off because you only want the notch to go halfway through the side. This corner piece must then be chiseled out completely. The length of your kickboard will be extended the thickness of one side of the couch. This will compensate for your notch on each end.

Chapter 7

Chair

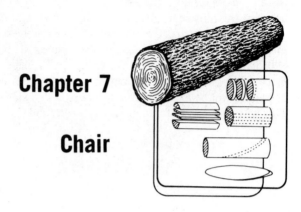

The basic construction techniques for the sofa also apply to the chair. There are a few added considerations that can make a chair blend more harmoniously with a sofa. Because of the length of the couch or love seat, you can put high sides on it and it can look beautiful. If you put matching high sides on the chair, it might look odd because it is much narrower.

Each piece must have its own inherent beauty, but it must also blend to form a set that balances. What you can get away with on the couch might be too heavy for a chair. You might have to build the chair with just a kickboard on all sides. You might have to use thinner wood for the sides of the chair. For example, if the sides of your sofa are 6-inch stock, you will have to go to three-inch stock for your chair. Keep in mind the size of a chair as compared to the couch and how the same wood will make it look. I have always had good luck with higher sides on the couch than on the chair. See Figs. 7-1 and 7-2.

There are some common measurements that should be adhered to for all chairs. The seat should be 16 to 17 inches off the floor. You can go an inch lower for a lounge chair and an inch higher for a typing chair. The width of the chair can vary according to need and design (from 17 to 30 inches or larger). The depth of the seat can vary from 15 to 23. This is dictated by design. The normal dimensions are for a 23-inch square cushion that measures 16 inches, top to floor. You can't go wrong with those numbers.

Fig. 7-1. Pine living room chair with kickboard on three sides.

Fig. 7-2. This chair has low sides.

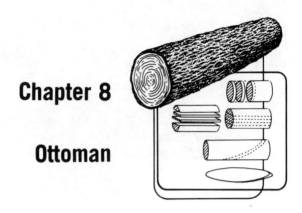

Chapter 8

Ottoman

An ottoman might be just the little touch you need to highlight your new set of furniture. The sides could match the chair in style or the boards could be cut down to a smaller width. The free edge could be on the bottom only with the cushion sitting in it.

The easiest way to make it is to construct a 2-×-4 frame and put the free-form boards on it. You can mitre the corners or butt them. The only really important thing is to make it not too high. The top of the cushion should be no more than 16 inches off the floor. The width and length are up to you. If you make it too large, it will look like a chair without a back.

If this is what you want (the modern style), make it the same dimensions as the chair; you can't go wrong. Most ottomans are 16 to 18 inches wide, 20 to 24 inches long and 15 to 16 inches high.

The lighter you want it to look, the more narrow you make the free-form boards. For example, your chair kickboard could be 11 inches and you could very easily make the ottoman 4 to 6 inches and still have it match.

I once cut a 1½″ strip off a board I used for the front of a couch and used it for an ottoman. The size of the ottoman was determined by how much I got out of the one strip I had. I then built it up to 15 inches with foam and I covered it. It was just what the room needed. See Fig. 8-1.

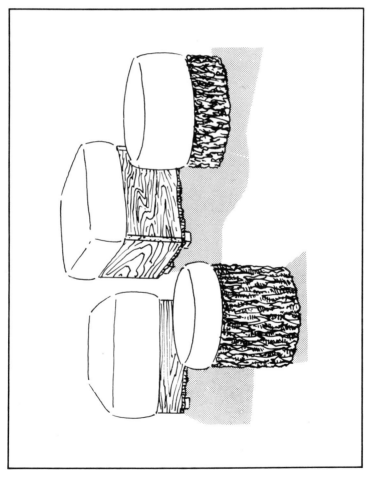

Fig. 8-1. Various ideas for making an ottoman.

47

Chapter 9

Gun Cabinet

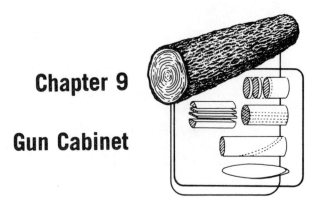

A gun cabinet is a very good piece of furniture to fit into a period room. Gun cabinets, by design, can be made as rustic looking as the pioneers made them.

The size and style of the cabinet is up to you. Size will be dictated by the number of guns you want to store and the space in which you must fit the cabinet. See Table 9-1. Decide first what you need or want.

■ What wood will you use, what you have, and what you can afford?

■ How many guns will it hold?

■ Will you need a storage cabinet at the bottom or will a drawer do—maybe neither?

■ How about the glass? Do you want sliding glass (or plexi-glass) doors, one large door that opens, or two smaller doors that both open?

■ What kind of legs do you want on it—if any?

■ What finish do you want? Stain or plain, glossy, or satin, oil or varnish?

Get some furniture catalogs, study the doors, drawers and cabinets, legs and get the overall picture. Finish reading this chapter. Then either use the basic design here or change it to suit your taste or needs.

I have a friend whose behavior is typically unorthodox in just about everything he does. He bought a standard double-door cabinet from a department store. It holds 10 guns. He took the racks out of one side and replaced them with racks to hang glasses and shelves to hold bottles. He now has a gun cabinet with a bar on one side and the guns on the other. Great idea if you like to sit around and drink while you talk about the 12-pointer that you almost got.

The following is a description of how to make the cabinet shown in Fig. 9-1. The cabinet will hold six guns and have a single plexiglass door.

SIDES

First make the sides. Select the two slabs that are the same thickness and close in overall dimension. Perhaps you can come up with a matchbook pair. After you have studied your boards and decided how wide you want the top and bottom, lay out the sides so that the bevel on each free edge will roll to the outside of the cabinet. The wider side of each board will be the inside wall of the cabinet.

In making the sides, I chose to square off the back so that it would sit neatly against the wall. I felt that getting rid of the free edge on the back would accentuate the front edge more. I wanted the bottom wider at the cabinet area than the top. This resembles the general shape of a conventional gun cabinet.

Lay out the lines on the sides. Be careful to cut the matching sides of each board. Don't cut off the free edge of one board and the opposite edge of the other.

I suggest you lay out the sides in the following fashion. Along the front edge, select the portion of the board you want to use. For

Table 9-1. Gun Cabinet Dimensions.

Gun Cabinet For Six Guns

Height: 74″
Depth: 13 1/2″
Width: 26″

Gun Cabinet For Eight Guns

Height: 74″
Depth: 12 1/2″—13 1/2″
Width: 31″

Gun Cabinet For Ten Guns

Height: 74″
Depth: 12 1 /2″—13 1 /2″
Width: 37″

Fig. 9-1. The gun cabinet.

instance, if your plank is 8 feet long and your cabinet will be 6 feet long, you might want to use the bottom portion on the plank rather than the top. Your decision might be prompted by the width of the bottom or the curvature of the free-form edge.

Assuming you want to square off the back, strike a chalk line the length of the board exactly where you want to make your cut. This will give you a line to work off with your T-square. Mark the line that will be the bottom cut. Along this chalk line, measure the desired length of the side and, again with a T-square, draw the line for the top cut. Look it over. If it is what you want, cut it out. You could use this side for a pattern to mark out the other side. These sides are 74″ × 13½″. Cut this side out and sand both sides of both pieces.

Your next step is plan ahead a bit. When you put the back on the cabinet, you definitely do not want merely to nail it to the back of the sides. This would make the back boards visible when looking at a side view. You want them hidden from the side view and so you must recess them. This is easy.

First measure the thickness of the boards you intend to use for your back. Mine were ¾″ thick. Set your sides up the way they will be in the finished product. Place the free edge in the front rolling to the outside. You want to cut a groove (rabbet) the whole length of each side piece. See Fig. 9-2 to get the idea.

When you are using a table saw, set the blade to a height of about half the thickness of your side board. It should be close to ½″. Set the fence for the exact thickness of the boards you will use on the back. Lay the side on the flat side and cut both side pieces on the

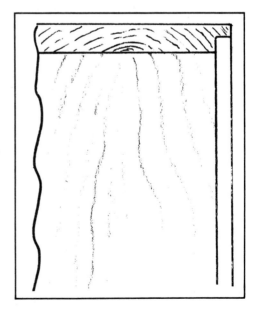

Fjig. 9-2. A dado joint.

inside back. Now set the height of the blade the exact thickness of the back boards and the fence to half the thickness of the sides. Turn the side board on end and run it through. The blade should be dead center and meet your other cut. Cut both and you have your rabbet.

If you are using a hand-held circular saw, make your cut exactly three-fourths of an inch, or the thickness of your back piece, in from the straightedge back and to a depth of half the thickness of the side piece. Use a 1 × 3 clamped into place as a fence. Make a series of cuts parallel to this cut and about ⅛″ apart, the full width of the rabbet. Clean with a chisel.

SHELVES

You need a top and bottom shelf for the cabinet and a middle shelf to set the guns on. They will all be the same width (side to side). They can all be a different depth (front to back) and they can also be different thicknesses. This sample cabinet has a 2″ top and bottom shelf and the middle shelf is 3″ thick.

Decide whether you want your shelves flush against the sides or whether you want to groove out the sides a bit (dado) and have them inserted into the side piece (see Fig. 9-3). If you decide to make them flush, just mark the sides wherever you want the shelves to be positioned. The shelves, in this case, will be exactly as wide as you want the inside of the cabinet.

If you want the dado effect, then cut the groove anywhere from ¼″ deep to half the thickness of the side. If, just for example, your dado is ½″ deep on each side, add this amount or 1″ to the inside dimension that you want and you have the width of the shelf. The width of the shelves in the cabinet shown is 32″.

Construction. Snap a chalk line along the free edge that you want showing in the front. Use a T-square to draw the sides. Now you must square the back of the shelf so that it will fit snugly against the back of the cabinet. Take the width of the side at the position of the shelf and subtract the thickness of the back you intend to use. This allows for the back of the cabinet to be recessed into the sides and your shelf to fit snugly against it. When you cut out all three shelves, each will have the same width, but each will probably have a different depth.

Attaching the Shelves. When you attach the shelves to the sides, it is crucial that you get them straight and level. Measure *exactly* 3″ down from the top of each side. Draw a line using the T-square off the back to mark your new line. This line will be the top of your shelf. Mark this line on both the inside and outside of the

Fig. 9-3. A dado joint for a shelf.

side pieces. Now measure the width of the shelf (after it is planed and sanded). Draw the line for the bottom of the shelf about 1/32″ less than the shelf thickness. This will give you a tight fit for your shelves if you use a dado. The depth of your dado should be no more than ½″ or, if your side is less than 1″ thick, no more than one-half the thickness of the side.

For the bottom shelf, measure 3″ from bottom of your side pieces. This line will be the *bottom* of your shelf. Repeat the same procedure as you used with the top shelf.

Now for the middle shelf. Measure 51″ down the side from the *bottom* of the upper shelf. Draw the line with a T-square. Do the same for the other side. This line will be the *top* side of your middle shelf. Draw the bottom line for the shelf a hair smaller than the width of that shelf. Measuring from the top of side to the top of this shelf, you can draw the shelf on the outside face of the cabinet sides. All three shelves are marked top and bottom on both faces of the side pieces. See Fig. 9-3.

CUTTING DADO JOINTS FOR SHELVES

Adjust the blade of your circular saw to the depth you need and use a bridge (a 2 × 4 or something clamped to the side) to serve as a guide for your saw when you make the cut. See Fig. 9-4.

Make the cut on the inside of each line you draw. Recheck the thickness. If it is too narrow, adjust the bridge and make another cut. Make full passes with the saw about ⅛″ apart between the top and bottom cut. Remove the waste with a sharp chisel. Do this for each side of the shelf.

When attaching the shelves, decide whether you will use screws, dowels or both. If your side pieces are 1″ thick or more, you can use screws that are countersunk about ½″ and put short dowels over them. Decide what screws you will use to secure the shelves. They should be flat heads and about 2½″ long. On the outside face of your side pieces, in the exact middle of each shelf, mark a spot 1″ in from each end and mark another spot in the exact center. These are the centers of your screw holes.

Center punch the point with a regular center punch or a large nail or screw. First drill a hole ½″ deep for your dowel. I suggest that you use a ½″ dowel and drill with a ½″ bit. Put a piece of masking tape or electrical tape (an adhesive bandage if you have no tape) around the bit ½″ up the shank. This will serve as a depth gauge so that you do not drill too deep. Drill these dowel holes first for all three shelves and on both side pieces.

Because the point of the drill bit is shaped like a V, you need not further center punch these holes. Select a drill bit the same size as the shank of the screws and drill in the center of the ½″ hole and rest of the way through the side. Do this with all the holes. Do this no matter whether you dado the sides or not.

Lay the cabinet side in a position that would place the cabinet

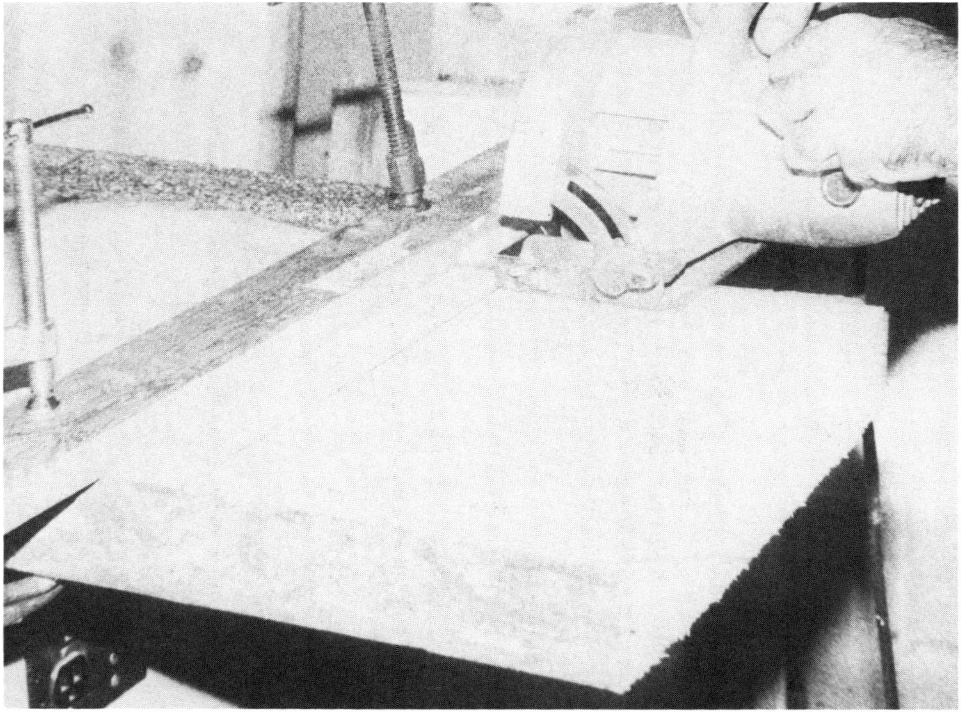

Fig. 9-4. Using a saw guide with a circular saw.

Fig. 9-4. Using a saw guide with a circular saw.

on its back. Place the top shelf in position using carpenter's glue; clamp it with furniture clamps. If you must persuade the shelf into the dado slot with a hammer, be sure to use a piece of buffer 2 × 4 and do not strike the side of the shelf with the hammer head.

If you are using soft wood such as pine, you need not drill pilot holes into the sides of the shelf because the screws will go in easily without them. For harder woods such as cherry, walnut, or oak, pilot holes and placing a liberal amount of soap on the screw are good ideas. Before you put the pilot holes or screws in, make doubly sure that the shelf is square and aligned front and back, top and bottom. Drive the screw tight leaving the ½" or so for your dowel.

Attach all shelves with glue and screws. At this point, square the whole cabinet and secure it. Nail 2 × 4s to the bench or prop a couple of full cases of beer against it to hold it until the glue dries.

ATTACHING THE BACK

The boards used on the back should be the same length as the side boards. In the example shown, I chose to cut the free edge off and butt the boards together. I picked two boards about the same width, cut the free edge off each and ended up with the boards the exact same width. I used these as the center boards because they were the widest I had. Take the exact measurement of the width across the back. The back will set inside the slot you cut out of the side piece (rabbet). Your measurement will take in the rabbet on both sides.

In this cabinet, I needed 3½" on each side to give me 31¼" width of the back. Having cut these (free edge off each piece), I had the whole back (in a pile) and was ready to put it together. What you want to do is butt the pieces together and put a couple of braces across the boards in the areas that the shelves will not brace. I suggest that you use boards 3 to 4" wide and about ¾" thick. The harder the wood you use for these braces the better.

Butt all boards together. Place carpenters' glue in the joints and secure with furniture clamps. Cut two braces to a length of about 2" shorter than the width of the back boards. The position of these boards is determined by the distance between the top and middle shelf. Divide the distance by three and place the braces of this interval between the two shelves. See Fig. 9-5.

Attach with glue and screws. Place the screws as shown in Figure 9-6. You should put them near (within an inch) the seams of the boards to be held together. Also a screw in the middle of each board helps to retard warping. When the back is completely dry, it is a good idea to attach it to the cabinet as soon as possible so that it doesn't sit around for weeks and warp. Remember the shelves will be part of the bracing for these boards.

When you attach the back, be sure the whole cabinet is square. Get the top and bottom even when you set it in place. Put some glue on the rabbet of the side pieces and a little across the back edge of

Fig. 9-5. Braces across the back.

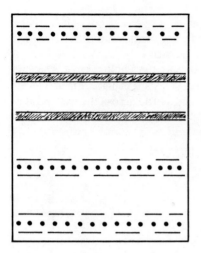

Fig. 9-6. Screws through the back
into the shelves.

each shelf. Hold it in place with a few, not too large, anchor-fast nails
into the sides. Measure again on the front where the shelves are and
mark them on the back so that you know where to put the screws.
Use narrow shank screws to hold the sides. Put screws across the
back into the shelves as indicated in Fig. 9-6.

As an option for the back you might prefer to use a piece of ½"
plywood finished on one side with a veneer to match the rest of your
cabinet.

Remember to let the cabinet dry for the time recommended for
the glue.

RACKS

Having gone this far in your construction, where everything is
finished except the doors and the racks, I suggest that you stain and
finish the cabinet before you put the remainder together. It is a lot
easier to stain and varnish the interior of the cabinet before the
racks and doors are secured in place. This gives you the freedom of
long clean strokes and less obstacles for stain or varnish to build up
around.

You want roughly 3" *between* the slots (both top and bottom).
The slots themselves are 2" wide. Measure the inside width of the
cabinet. Let's assume it is 31" wide and a 6-gun cabinet. See Fig.
9-7.

Top Rack. Cut the top rack 31" wide and 2½" deep. I left the
free form edge on the front of both racks. Get the center point of the
width (15½" from each end). This point is the center of the 3" space
between the three guns on the left and the three on the right.

Measure 1½″ off the center to each side and you have your middle spaces. With a T-square (always with a T-square), mark the lines. Go another 2″ off each line. These are your two center slots. Connect these lines that are 2″ apart with a rough semicircle just to keep things straight. You can square them up with a compass later.

Measure 3″ spacers and the 2″ holes until you have all six holes drawn. You should have 2″ left over on each end. Perfect. Now draw a line 1¼″ from the *back* of the rack. This line is the back of your 2″ slot because the barrel holder should be only 1″ to 1½″ deep. I chose to use 1¼″ because it seems to make a nice comfortable nest for the barrel.

Round the back of the slot with a compass. All of the slots should now be uniformly 2″ wide and 1¼″ deep. With this piece you are free to tailor the width for your particular guns if you so choose. All mine are single barrel except one. This is an old double-barrel gun that measures 1¾″ across the both barrels.

I made the slots all 2″ so that it will fit in any slot I happen to put it. If all your guns are single barrel and you want to make these slots 1¼″ or 1½″, feel free to do so.

Be careful to keep the center of the smaller top slot directly over the 2″ bottom slot that will hold the stock. I suggest that you lay both out for 2″ and from that pattern slim down the top ones to what you want.

When you get the piece all laid out and you have double-checked the measurements, cut out the slots. Take your time! Use a hand-held coping saw, an electric jig saw or a hand-held electric saber saw. Go slow and be neat. Save the pieces you cut out. They might (or might not) be useful if you glue felt in the slot. You might be able to stick them back to hold the felt tight until the glue dries.

Bottom Rack. Right now you must make a decision. Do you want the bottom rack, which sets on the middle shelf, to be positioned in the middle of the shelf or to extend from the very back of the cabinet and cover almost the whole shelf. The front of the rack

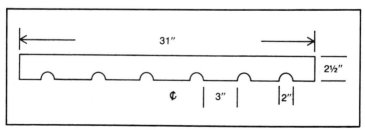

Fig. 9-7. A top rack to hold barrels.

Fig. 9-8. Comparison of slot to barrel size.

should be about 9½ or 9¾" from the back of the cabinet. The slots should be about 6½" deep and 2" wide. This should be plenty large enough to hold the butt of any gun.

The back of this rack need not touch the back of the cabinet, but it could sit in the middle of the shelf and save you from worrying about an absolutely perfect fit in the corners. The rack should be at least 7½" deep. This gives you an inch of solid wood behind the slots. Cut the rack 31" wide and 7½ to 9½" deep (depending on what you want). Place the finished top rack on the bottom one so that the round part of the 2" slot rests 6½" from the front edge of the bottom. See Fig. 9-9.

Draw the slots and remove the top rack. Extend the straight lines to the front of the bottom rack and check the measurements. Cut out the 6½ × 2" slots.

Sand, stain, and finish (varnish or whatever) both racks. Glue felt in the slots if you so prefer. You can use the pieces you cut out of the slots to hold the felt secure until the glue dries (Fig. 9-10).

Installation. When you position the bottom rack, make absolutely sure that the front is 9½" from the back of the cabinet. You can fasten it in place by glue only (pile a few heavy books on it until it dries) or by putting a few screws in it (countersink them and plug the holes or screw up from the underneath of the shelf).

The barrel rack should be about 32" above the bottom rack and fastened snug against the back of the cabinet. Measure the height and make sure it is not crooked. Mark it. Drill 3 pilot holes for the screws through the back wall of the cabinet. Drill from the inside so that you are sure to be right in the middle of the rack. Position the rack and screw it in place. You don't need to glue it if you use screws.

If you prefer you can use only glue. If you do this, lay the cabinet on its back so that the glue won't run all over the place. You can either glue or screw this piece because it won't be supporting any weight.

BOTTOM DOORS

Construction. The double doors at the bottom of the cabinet will be attached to the sides by hinges and have a clearance of about 1/32" from the bottom and middle shelf. Cut the doors to exact size on three sides and make the width of the doors wide enough that the free edges will come within about ½ to 1" of each other.

Study Figs. 9-11 and 9-12 and have a clear picture of what you want before you cut anything. For this cabinet, I left the free edge on one side of the doors. You need not do this. You can cut all sides and have the doors touch in the middle when closed or keep the separation if you like. Decide what you want and cut both doors the same dimension with the grain running the same way.

At this point I prefer to "overkill" a bit. I like to put braces on the doors to help insure against warping. Run the braces across the

Fig. 9-9. The bottom rack.

Fig. 9-10. The inside of the cabinet after it has been stained.

grain (2 on each door) and to within an inch of each edge of the door. Don't run the braces the full width of the door because they might get in the way of its closing properly. Use both glue and screws to attach these. Sand, stain, and finish the doors before you put them on.

62

Attaching the Doors. One method is to use a solid piece as a brace for the door. Run the grains the opposite way from the door. See Fig. 9-12.

When you attach the doors to the side wall of the cabinet, as was done in the model for this chapter, you must use either a butt hinge, as I did, or the pin type that fits on the top and bottom of the door. Keep in mind that the sides of the cabinet are wider at the bottom and you want the doors to hang plumb. You can do this in two ways.

■ Measure from the inside back of the cabinet the same distance to the top and bottom of the door. Mark it. Do the same for the other door.

■ Plumb the whole cabinet with a level. Be especially careful

Fig. 9-11. Braces for the bottom door.

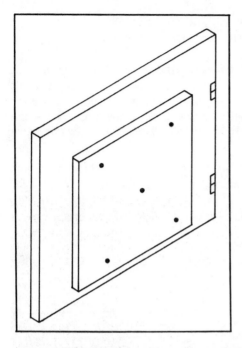

Fig. 9-12. An alternate brace for the bottom door.

that the back is true. Then place a door about where you want it. Plumb that with a level. Mark it. I suggest you measure first. Then check with the level.

Put the hinges on the doors first. Fold the butt hinge in the position it will be when the door is closed. You want to recess the hinge into the door the distance of the total thickness of the complete hinge (not just one side but both sides). Trust me. This will enable the door to be flush with the side of the cabinet when closed.

This method is much easier than trying to recess each side of the hinge. The easiest way to recess the hinge is to use a sharp chisel. It's not that deep. The only thing visible then is the pin of the hinge. Think about buying butt hinges with a fancy pin. At any rate, try to get larger hinges for the larger top door than you get for the smaller storage doors. This might not be possible if you don't have the time to run all over and look for them. Once the hinges are attached to the doors, screw the other side of the hinge to the side of the cabinet. Make sure the screws are not too long and there is no danger of them going all way through the side.

Now that the doors are in place, you might want to put a post in the middle to cover any space left between the doors. Make the post the exact length of the distance between the shelves. Make it fit

Fig. 9-13. The center post between bottom doors.

snug. Make it wide enough to completely cover the opening, but not much wider. Position it so that the doors fit tightly against it and that they are even across the front. They should not close too far or not enough. You can fasten this with a couple of finishing nails through each side into the top and bottom shelf. Countersink them and fill.

Put a couple of magnets under the middle shelf and on each side of the post. The plate will be on the door itself. You buy these magnets the same place you get the hinges. Place the knobs on the post side of the doors. Make sure they are *outside* the post area or else the screw for the knob will hit the post and keep the door from shutting all the way. See Fig. 9-13.

Top Door. Once again you have a number of options when planning what type of door you will use. Glass or plexiglass? Free edge on the inside or plain? For that matter, one or two doors? Use two if you want.

Glass is less expensive than plexiglass, less durable, won't scratch like plexiglass, and it is a bit more work to install. Glass needs a frame to hold it. Plexiglass can be drilled and screwed into place without a frame. On the other hand, plexiglass should always be cleaned with a plexiglass polish. I used plexiglass mainly because my nieces and nephews will be around and I felt it was safer without glass. That was rather spurious reasoning because there are also windows and sliding-glass doors in the same room.

I also went with the free edge on the inside for two reasons. I had enough boards left over to get the free edge form and I thought it would look really sharp. I did like it very much when it was finished. Without the extra wood, I would have made another door without the free form. Another factor to consider is that the corners of the free form are a bit more difficult because you rarely have matching pieces. Therefore, you cannot just mitre the joints. We'll see this in more detail later.

One or two doors? I chose one door because I was afraid that, with the free edge, two doors would be just a bit too much "ginger bread." Had I used plain doors, I might have gone with two. Another factor to keep in mind is that the cabinets for six guns usually have one door; eight guns or more usually have two doors.

For this particular cabinet of six guns, I am happy with my choice of a single, free-edge, plexiglass door.

Construction. Take your planks and measure the desired length you want. Do it in this way to be safe. Your free edge will wander in and out so stretch a string line along the free edge so that the curves are rather uniform all along the string line. See Fig. 9-14.

Measure the width you want (let's say 2″). Strike the line. Cut to the *full* length of the opening between top and middle shelf. Do this for all four sides of your door. Make each piece 1/16″ shorter than you need. Now measure the short pieces and make them also 1/16″ smaller than you need. I used a lap joint for the corners. See Fig. 9-15.

Half the thickness is cut from each piece. Place the long side over (on top of) the top and bottom pieces. Square the corners and mark the short side on the face. Flip the whole thing over, square it again, and mark the back of the long sides. Cut half way through each piece and then cut lengthwise in the center of the board down to the cut. In this cabinet, I merely glued the joints and clamped them until they were completely dry.

I realized the plexiglass screwed to the back would help support the corners and give the door some rigidity. To improve the appearance of the door, I drilled two holes through each lap joint. The size of the holes I drilled was determined by the size of the dowels I had on hand. These happened to be ⅜″ dowels, and I thought they would be about the right size for this joint. I glued the dowels and let them dry. Then I sanded them flush on both sides. I

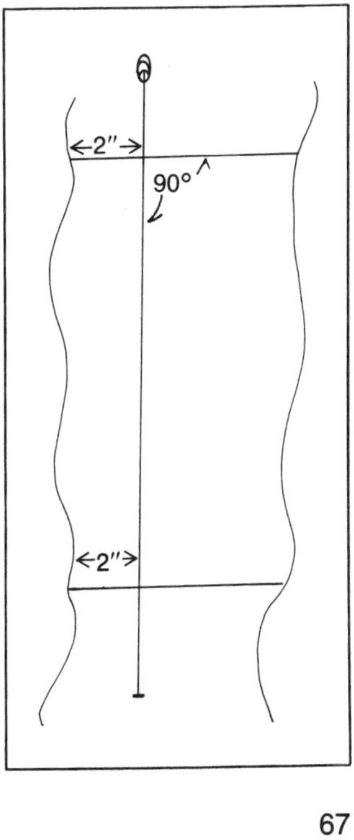

Fig. 9-14. A string line for measuring the straight edge of doors.

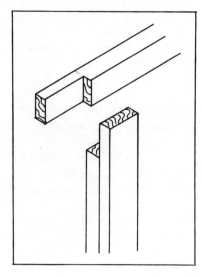

Fig. 9-15. A lap joint for doors.

sanded, stained, and put the finish on the door before I did anything else. Don't forget to do the edges because you will see them when the door is open.

I bought the plexiglass cut to size. I ordered the piece about 1½″ smaller in length and width than the finished door frame. This allowed the glass to be about ¾ of an inch recessed all around the door.

Attach the plexiglass to the inside of the door with small screws. Drill the plexiglass first. Have one screw in each corner, one in the center of the top and bottom, and two or three down each side.

Attach the hinges in the same way as described for the bottom doors. Recess the hinge in the door and when you hang it make sure it's plumb. Add the door handle and magnets on top and bottom.

There is one touch you might want to add. On the very top of the back, above the top shelf, I put a piece of free-form wood against the back and extended it a bit above the back (see Fig. 9-1). This is just trim and you can skip it if you like.

Your gun cabinet is finished. Take a good look at it and see if anything is missing.

Chapter 10
Grandfather Clock

This style of clock is rather unorthodox. It lacks the ornateness of the traditional old chime clock and it keeps with the Early American flavor of Shaker. My intention in building this was to make a clock to match the gun cabinet described in Chapter 9. I also wanted to show that it is possible to break from tradition and produce an elegant piece of furniture.

I started by studying the clocks my friends have in their homes. Most were made from precut kits they had purchased from mail-order houses and put together themselves. They were very nice but not my style. I don't like kits any more than I like to paint by number.

I gathered a variety of dimensions and formulated the dimensions for the case. I ordered the chime and clock movement from a mail-order house. I waited until it arrived before I started to make sure it would fit within the size case I had planned. It fit with a few inches to spare and I decided to go with my original measurements rather than cut it down. I was afraid it would look undernourished.

Much of this clock was made exactly as described in the gun cabinet. The sides, top, bottom shelf, and back are made exactly the same as are the two doors. Only the dimensions change. The construction is exactly the same.

SIDES

The boards I had were 1½" stock planed to 1⅜". For the back I use ½" stock. The boards are 74" tall and 11" deep. I refer you to the

Table 10-1. Grandfather Clock Dimensions.

Height:	74″
Width:	17½″
Depth:	11″
Stock:	1½″ planed to 1⅜″
Back:	½″ stock
Shelf Below Mechanism:	1¾″ stock

section on sides in Chapter 9. For this clock, even the dimensions are about the same. The back is squared off as are the top and bottom. The free edge is in the front with the bevel rolling to the outside. I tried to make this a carbon copy of the gun cabinet. Someone did mention that if I no longer wanted the gun cabinet I could cut it in half and make two more clocks out of it.

After you make the sides and completely sand them on both faces (I mean completely—all the way down to the fine paper and pumice), Cut the grooves (dado) in for the top and bottom shelf only. Cut the rabbet for the back. As for the gun cabinet, the back is recessed. These grooves will be cut about ½″ deep into the sides. In the clock cabinet, I used full shelves for the top and bottom. For the middle two shelves, I used only 3″ deep fake shelves. The reason is that you need the unobstructed space from the top to the bottom of the clock for the clock mechanism, pendulum, and weights.

I did not cut a dado for these shelves. You could do so if you like. I merely glued them in place. If you are not pressed for time, I suggest that you cut a dado with a chisel and recess these pieces. It makes for a more uniform appearance. Remember to make the dado the thickness of the shelves you will use and not cut the dado to the dimensions given here.

SHELVES

The width of the shelves will determine the width of the clock cabinet. Remember to subtract the width of the sides and add the depth of each dado. This determines the width of the shelves. Make doubly sure both are the same size. The depth of the shelves if the same as the sides *less* the depth of the rabbet so that the back can be recessed. Sand the inside surface of each shelf.

Secure the shelves in place with carpenters' glue and countersink the screws through the sides into each shelf. Glue fake dowels over the screw heads (as in the gun cabinet). Make sure that the whole thing is square.

Fig. 10-1. The grandfather clock.

In the gun cabinet, the top shelf is 2" from the top and the bottom shelf is 2" from the floor. In the clock cabinet, the top shelf is 2" from the top, but the bottom shelf is 3" up from the floor. It is recommended that some weight be put in the bottom of the case for stability because the clock mechanism, especially when the weights are up, tends to make the whole thing top heavy. I chose to bolt steel plates under the bottom shelf (between it and the floor) rather than put anything on that shelf because this steals space from inside the cabinet.

This space might be needed for an eight-day clock. In order for the mechanism to run a full eight days, the weights are pulled down sometimes to within a half inch of the bottom shelf. There is more about installing the steel at the end of this chapter.

FAKE SHELVES

As you can see in Fig. 10-1, there looks to be a shelf at the bottom of the clock and one at the top of the compartment at the base of the cabinet. They're fake. The top one is 3" deep and the bottom one is 2½" deep, showing the free edge in front. Cut them both to length and sand them completely. I constructed the bottom assembly first (Fig. 10-2). This consists of the panel that encloses the lower portion of the cabinet. See Fig. 10-2.

I simply made the panel solid with no free-form edges because I felt, with the free edges surrounding it on all four sides, any more would have been too much. I didn't bother to make this panel open (a door) because the space cannot be used for storage anyway.

Cut the panel to size and sand. If you have a choice you might want to make the grain run top to bottom. I didn't happen to have a board large enough so I ran the grain side to side. Use carpenters' glue on all four sides, position the board carefully in place, and tap it down by holding a piece of 2 × 4 on top.

Using a small T-square, make sure this wood is squared off the bottom shelf. You can hold it firm with a few finishing nails diagonally through the back, side, and into the sides and bottom. Make sure they don't come through.

Now glue the "fake" lower shelf on top of this board and add a finishing nail through the back into each side. The bottom board cannot be too deep because, if the mechanism is far forward, the weights will hit it on the way down and stop the clock (2½" was fine on mine). If they hit when yours is finished, trim the board with a sabre saw.

Position the other "fake" shelf at the bottom of the clock

mechanism. Here I used 1¾" stock (mainly because it was all I had). Glue the shelf in place. Use a small T-square off the side. Make sure that it is not crooked. Tack it from the back if you prefer.

BACK

The back of the clock differs from that of the gun cabinet in that the back of the clock mechanism should be open and accessible after the permanent back is put on. See Fig. 10-3. This allows necessary access to the chime lock and other parts.

A removable panel is used to secure this area. The back will extend from the floor upward to within 18" of the top shelf. This will give you room to install the mechanism. Because the clock is rather narrow, you might have one board that will cover the complete width. I was not so lucky and had to piece the distance across with three boards.

I put the largest board dead center and the two smaller on each side. If you have to use this technique, glue the edges, butt, and

Fig. 10-2. The lower panel.

clamp with furniture clamps. Secure three braces across the boards. Glue and screw these braces in place. For braces, use a hard wood, if possible, such as oak or maple. Pine will give you little protection against the back warping because the moving wood is strong enough to bend the pine easily.

I stained the braces, shown in Fig. 10-3, for your easy identification. The removable panel is also stained to differentiate it from the back. Allow it to dry for 24 hours and sand the side that will be visible from the front of the cabinet. Position the back in place with glue and nails. I placed a few thin 1¼" wood screws about every 12" apart to secure it well.

DOORS

I used a 2" wide border for each door. When you measure this, make the *widest* part of the irregular edge the full 2". Refer to the section on doors in Chapter 9 and make both doors the same way. I would suggest that you leave about 1/16" space around each side of the doors in order to allow for expansion.

When the doors are completely finished, sand them thoroughly on both sides before adding hardware. Use two butt hinges on each door and countersink them in the door rather than the side of the cabinet or partially in both.

You can use glass or plexiglass in these doors. Glass can be secured with a molding or with mirror hangers. Plexiglass can be installed the same way because you can drill through it and simply use small screws to hold it in place. I suggest screws for the top piece because you will not want the face recessed any more than necessary. Molding and hangers take up room. You can install the doors at this point if you like. I waited until after I stained and finished the cabinet to install plexiglass in the doors.

REMOVABLE PANEL

Measure the distance from the upper edge of the top shelf down to the back. Use the wood you have made the cabinet from or simply cut a piece of plywood (I used ½" plywood) to fit. This will not be seen from the front at all. You can secure it with four screws or with small pieces of wood that turn back and forth to hold or release. See Fig. 10-3.

I cut ½"-×-½" strips into 1½" lengths and merely nailed them on the sides. They are not tight enough that they won't turn and yet just tight enough that they stay where you put them. These will hold the back in place. See Figs. 10-3 and 10-4.

Fig. 10-3. The back of the clock.

Fig. 10-4. The removable panel on the back.

STAIN AND FINISH

At this point I completely stained and finished the cabinet. The stain is Provincial and the finish is a rubbed high-gloss polyurethane.

INSTALLING THE CLOCK MECHANISM

Your clock will consist of the brass mechanism permanently mounted in a hardwood box-type frame (almost like a shadow box). It might also have two pieces of ¼" plywood stapled to that frame and extending up the sides between the works and the face of the clock.

Fig. 10-5. The backing board behind the brass face.

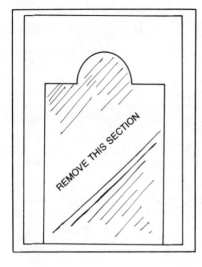

Fig. 10-6. A sketch of a three-sided backing board.

REMOVE THIS SECTION

If the door in front of the face will cover all but the brass, you can leave these pieces of plywood on because they will not be seen. But if they show, remove them . . . very carefully. Pry the staples out first and the pieces will come off.

Now you must make a piece for in back of the face that extends from side to side and from the top to the fake shelf at the base of the mechanism. Because it is difficult to make this to size and cut a hole in the middle and slide it over the face, I suggest you make it first to fit the space it will sit in and then cut out the middle area to fit over the mechanism and behind the face. If you cut away the bottom section, you will have three sides left and you can fit it behind the face with no problem. See Fig. 10-5.

The bottom section can be covered by the border of the door which comes up to the bottom of the brass. See Fig. 10-6. Allow a little play between this front panel and the wooden case of the movement so that you have room to balance the mechanism when you install it. In other words, make this backing piece fit loosely.

The next thing to consider is how you want to secure the face board you made. You can glue two ¾"-×-¾" strips down the sides and nail those to the sides of the cabinet. See Fig. 10-7. This necessitates that your front board be snug on all sides and the clock face be perfectly aligned and square on all sides. If your case is square all way around, this is not too difficult. If it is not square you will have problems.

Another way is to put a ⅝" molding around the opening so that it touches the back of the door at all points. This also gives you a solid stop for your door when you close it. I chose this method. Use ⅝″ molding because this gives you enough clearing for your clock face.

When making the molding, I used scraps of the same wood I made the cabinet from. Cut ⅝″-×-⅝″ strips on your circular saw. Sand the two sides that will show and round the edge between them. Cut the four sides to fit snugly. I used a mitre box and cut 45 degree corners. Stain and varnish them. Nail them in place. The door being shut to the position you want it will give you a guide as to exactly where the molding goes. Butt it against the door all way around. Glue and nail with wire brads.

If you use the molding method, you can make your faceplate about 1/16″ short on all sides. This gives you the leeway to move it around and get the face perfectly square.

Fit the faceplate in and adjust it. The clock will have to be on it for this. You will need four hands and four eyes for this. Remember, you still can adjust the clock within the leeway you left between the sides of the faceplate and the hardwood frame of the mechanism. Once you have the faceplate in place, tack the edges of the panel to the molding. Make sure the face is square.

The movement will sit on a wooden baseboard that is as long as the inside dimension of the cabinet and as wide as the hardwood housing for the mechanism. It will have a ⅝″ slot in the center that is as long as the mechanism. See Fig. 10-8. I suggest you use 1″ stock for this piece. Make it fit snugly.

When installing this piece *do not* remove the ties or rubber bands holding them together. Make sure the chains are not twisted on the sprockets. *Do not* remove the rubber band holding the pendulum arm secure.

Slide the base up. The chains should be hanging in the slot. Make the back of this board flush with the back of the hardwood frame. Use screws only (not glue) to secure the braces beneath the

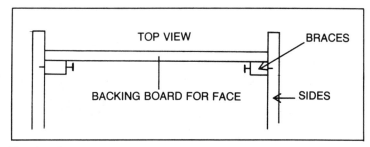

Fig. 10-7. Strips to secure the backing board to the side of the cabinet.

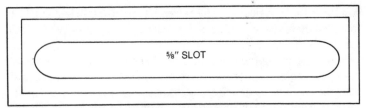

Fig. 10-8. A wooden base to hold the mechanism.

base to the sides. Put a couple of finish nails through the base into the braces. Leave them extend out about ½". Don't drive them flush. See Fig. 10-9.

You can glue the slotted base to the braces, but don't glue anything to the sides. This allows you to remove the works at a future date for oiling and possible repair. You can also put a drop of glue between the hardwood on the mechanism and your slotted base to hold it secure. Either that or glue small blocks to your slotted base to hold the mechanism in place.

INSTALLATION OF CHIMES

The instructions of your clock works will give you some directions (more than mine, I hope) as to how to install the chime rods. My instructions merely said install the rods so that the hammers hit dead center of each rod. I looked at other clocks and other instructions from people who have built them and found that the hammers

Fig. 10-9. The base and braces.

should strike ⅞" down from the bottom of the cast-iron housing that holds the rods. Here you need four hands again.

In making the board that holds the rods, make it as long as the inside of the cabinet and have a snug fit. Use 1" stock. Make it as wide as the cast iron that is to be mounted on it. Have someone hold it approximately in place as you hold the chim rods on it and mark where it goes. This will not necessarily be dead center of the board because the hammers are not dead center in the mechanism. Drill the four holes the size of the bolts supplied. Mount the chime rods.

I cut away part of the board so I would have a better view of the hammers when positioning this board in place. This helped a little but not much. I used a small mirror to see better while adjusting the hammers.

Secure the board in place with glue and toe nail it into the side. See Fig. 10-10. The instructions should tell you that if a hammer or two are not centered you can bend them with a pair of needle-nose pliers so that they hit the center of the rod and produce a clear note. Your clock should not sound like a bar room tenor.

STEEL WEIGHTS

Because the clock is naturally a bit top heavy, especially when the weights are all the way up, it is a good idea to add some weight in the bottom. You might get away with placing a few bricks in the back of the bottom compartment and the weights might not hit them

Fig. 10-10. The backing board for chimes.

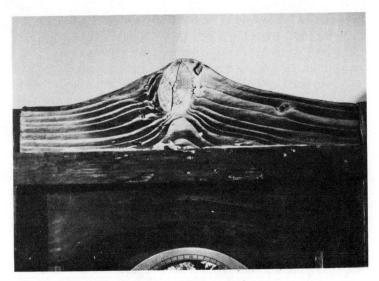

Fig. 10-11. The trim on top of the cabinet.

when they are fully down. I simply screwed a piece of ¼″ channel steel, 14″ long and 5″ wide, to the underside of the bottom shelf (between it and the floor). This provided sufficient weight for my clock.

As long as the chains are tied, you can lay the cabinet on its back and not hurt the mechanism. Don't turn it completely upside down. This will allow the chains to fall off the wheels and then you will have a problem getting them back on.

FINISHING TOUCHES

At this point, the clock matched the gun cabinet perfectly. But being a clock, it needed, I thought, some touch of its own to bring out it's personality. The top seemed to me unfinished. I'm sure my thinking was influenced by the look of traditional clocks. At the risk of destroying the perfect match, I cut the piece on the front above the top shelf from a board which I was lucky enough to have staring at me. I stained and finished it, and merely glued it into place. It seemed to me the perfect finishing touch. You might prefer to go with a careful match with the gun cabinet. Refer to Figures 10-1 and 10-11. The choice is yours.

Install the hardware, door handle, knob, and magnets to hold the doors shut. At this point, I moved the whole thing to the spot I intended to permanently keep it. At that point, I adjusted the hammers and hung the pendulum and weights. Don't forget to put on the back panel. I then carefully put it in the corner and leveled it.

From here on, you follow the manufacturers' directions in setting it, starting it, and setting the chimes to ring in the proper sequence. You now have a beautiful clock and a conversational piece. "I never saw one like it." Neither had I until it was finished.

Chapter 11

Storage Box

The chest is a useful storage item and can lend to the decor an added touch of elegance as well as utility. It can be used as a window seat or even a coffee table (if you leave the trim off the lid). The size can vary somewhat depending on the surroundings and purpose. You can make the box longer or shorter and even wider. Don't fool around too much with the depth or it will be no good as a table or a seat. The average size of a chest is about 17″ deep. They vary from 32″ to 42″ in length and 17″ to 19″ wide.

The chest shown in Fig. 11-1 was designed as a wood box to be used also as a window seat. It violates the dimensions given above because it was to stand somewhat alone in a spacious room with heavy furniture. Because of all of these factors the dimensions were stretched a bit.

Before you can begin, decide on the exact size you want. Let's assume you want a normal size chest (30″ × 19″ × 17″ high). Use ½″ boards for the sides and lid.

Cut a piece of ½″ plywood or ⅝ flake board exactly 29″ × 18″ Make sure that the corners are perfectly square. Line the bottom with 2 × 3s. You can use a simple butt joint or get a little more fancy.

If you use the butt joint, cut 2 pieces of 2 × 3s exactly 29″ long. Glue and screw them with the narrow side (2″) down. Position them flush with the edge of the front and back of your plywood. Next cut two pieces to fit in between the long 2 × 3s. They will be about 14½″ or so long. Position them with glue and screws. To be on the safe and strong side, put a screw, about every foot, through the plywood into the 2 × 3. Now strengthen the corners by putting a screw (or dowel) in each butt joint. Make sure the glue is in the joints as well as the flat surfaces.

SIDES

The free edge in this box will go around the bottom. It will completely cover the 2 × 3 and in some places extend a bit below the bottom edge of the 2 × 3. See Fig. 11-2.

You must be sure that the bottom is completely hidden by the sides. Because you want the box to be 17″ high, and you will put a lid on it, subtract the thickness of the boards you will use for the lid from the 17″, and this is how wide or tall your side pieces will be.

You need not use the same thickness boards for your lid as you use for your sides.

For example, you might have ½″ stock for the sides and enough ⅞″ for your lid. You can do this if you like. But for simplicity, let's assume you will use ½″ boards throughout. In other words, to measure the width of the front and back boards you subtract ½″ (which will be taken up later by the lid) from the 17″ and of course you get 16½″.

Because you want the box 30″ long, you build the frame 29″ so that the ½″ stock on each end will make up the 30″. So make the long side board 30⅛″ long, ½″ overhand on each end plus 1/16 more on each end will give you a chance to sand the box flush and smooth.

Mark the board in the following manner. Put a chalk line along the free edge. See Fig. 11-3. Use the chalk line to get your square corners as well as a base to measure up 16½ inches. Cut one of these if you intend to have your box against the wall. If on the other

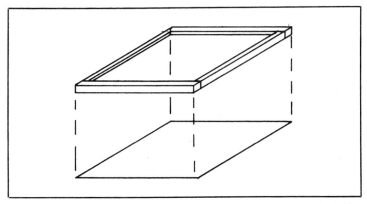

Fig. 11-1. A 2″-×-3″ bottom support with plywood attached to the underside.

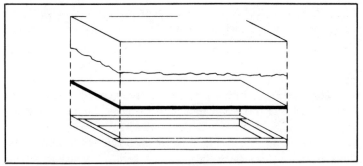

Fig. 11-2. A 2″-×-3″ bottom support with the plywood bottom resting on it.

hand, you might want to use it as a coffee table or end table. Then you want all sides to be finished so cut two pieces instead of one. If you will use it as a window seat against the wall, the back can be ½″ plywood or flake board.

In attaching the front (and back if you cut it), use the chalk line as your point of reference. The chalk line must go exactly along the bottom of the 2 × 3. You have an option here of attaching it by countersinking the screws through the face and plugging the holes with dowels or you can screw through the 2 × 3 into the inside part of the side boards. This is the method I used for attaching the boards to the bottom. I felt that the dowels so close to the free edge would detract from it. I used the countersink method for securing the butt joints of the sides.

Glue and screw the front piece onto the 2 × 3 and allow the overhang on each end. If you are using the free form on all four sides, attach the back in the same fashion. If you are finishing all four sides and you have the front and back in place, you need only to fill in the short sides. Strike the chalk line on the free edge and square off at 18″ wide and 16½″ high. Attach with glue and screws in the same way you did the other two sides.

If you are short of wood or if you need only three finished sides on your box, build the sides 18½″ wide instead of 18″ so that they

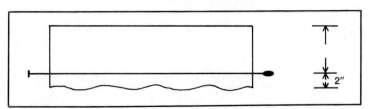

Fig. 11-3. Use a chalk line to acquire a straight free edge.

will extend ½″ beyond the back. This will hide the plywood you will use for the back side.

On the three-finished sided box, attach the short sides after you attach the front. Then put on a piece of ½″ plywood to fill in the back side.

Now that you have all four sides on, you need to fasten all the butt joints with screws before the glue dries. I will assume you are using ½″ dowels for a filler over the countersunk screws. First drill the pilot holes for the screws and then drill the ½″ holes for the dowels to the depth of ¼″ into the pilot holes. Put the screws in tight. Cut the dowels to a length of about ⅛″ longer than you need. Glue and tap them tight. When you sand the sides, you can sand the dowels flush.

THE LID

Decide how much you want the lid to hang over. I used 1 inch. The 1″ overhang is only in the front and sides of this box. If you use the box as a coffee table, have the overhang on all four sides.

If you do want the overhang on all four sides, you want the dimensions of the top to be 32 × 21″. Unless you have a 21″ wide board, you will have to piece the top together. More for that in a minute. I will assume, for simplicity, that you use one board 32″ × 21″. I used no hinges on the box I made with this type of lid. I merely used another piece of flake board 29″ × 18″ that fit inside the box. I screwed it exactly centered to the bottom of the 32″ × 21″ finished top. I set the top on and let the flake board hold it in place.

If you have to piece the top from two boards, because you don't have a 21″ wide hunk of tree, slice the free edge off of one side of each board and leave the trimmed slab 10½″ wide. Butt the trimmed edges together and glue and screw them to the flake board. Screw through the flake board into the top. Make the free edge flow so that you can see the wider part at the bottom.

If you are going to use this box as a window seat and if you have the top overhang on only three sides, your best bet is to square the back by removing the free edge. Then attach the top with butt hinges on the back. Notch out the area for each hinge about 9″ in from each end. If you use a single, solid board for the top, you need not use the 29-×-18 flake board on the underside of it. If you use two or more boards to make up the top, it would be a good idea to use the flake board underlay.

At this point you can quit while you're ahead or you can give it one more shot and add the final touch of "Early Americanism." This

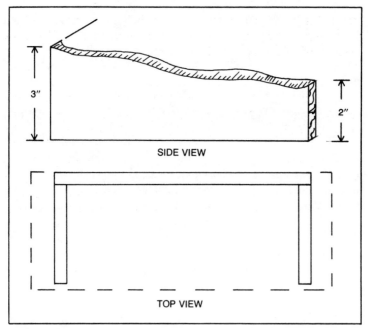

Fig. 11-4. Trim on the top of the chest.

applies only if you also want to make the box a seat. It looks much more classy if you frame the cushion (back and sides) with a little free-form touch. If you put a cushion on you don't want it to extend to the very edge of the lid.

For this box, make the back support about 3″ high and 28″ long. Leave the free edge on the top and have the bevel roll toward the front. Attach this board along the back edge, with glue and screws, through the bottom. If the width of this board was ½″, make the side pieces 18″ to 18½″ long (3″ in the back and tapering to 2″ in the front).

Attach the side pieces with the bevel rolling to the outside and the back butting against them. See Fig. 11-4. Glue and screw from the bottom. You might want to put a dowel or screw and dowel into the butt joint to hold it firm.

Before adding these pieces, you should completely sand the box. You might even stain the lid. I preferred to sand and stain all three pieces and the lid before I put them together. Make sure you finish both sides of your side pieces.

For the seat, get a 1″ or 2″ piece of foam rubber and cut it to size. I have found that an electric knife cuts as well as anything I have used. Hope you have one. All that is left is to cover the foam with a matched or contrasting fabric and you are ready to fill the box with wood, blankets or whatever.

Cedar. If you have a need for a cedar chest, you can line the box with cedar without too much trouble. There is available, at some, but not all, lumber yards a flake board that is made from cedar chips. Probably the best to buy is a 4-×-8 sheet of ¼" or, at most, ⅜" cedar flakeboard. One sheet will be plenty enough to line the box.

Instead of using plywood on the bottom, use cedar flakeboard. Do the same for the underlay of the lid. No matter whether you use a lid of one or more boards, use a base piece of cedar. After you make the bottom frame of 2 × 3s with the cedar board and then put your outside free form on it, adjust the dimensions as needed.

Now you have a storage chest, a hope chest, or a cedar chest. I hope the cedar keeps the moths out. On the other hand, you can put woolen items in a plastic bag, with a few moth balls, and protect them just as well. This lacks that nice cedar smell though.

Chapter 12

Tables

All tables that you sit at and eat from should be about 29 inches high and have at least a 24-inch clearance for your knees. See Fig. 12-1.

A table for two people should be about 24 inches in diameter. See Fig. 12-2.

A round table for four people should be 36 inches in diameter. See Fig. 12-3.

A square table for four people can be 32 inches. See Fig. 12-4.

A round table for six people should be at least 48 inches in diameter. See Fig. 12-5.

A rectangular table for six people should be 58 to 60 inches long and 36 inches wide. See Fig. 12-6.

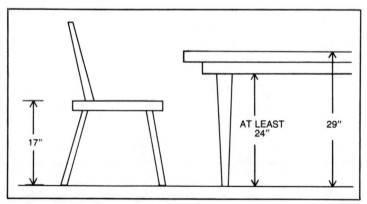

Fig. 12-1. Height of average table and chair.

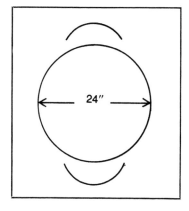

Fig. 12-2. Table for Two (Round)

A rectangle for eight people should be 82 inches long and 36 inches wide. See Fig. 12-7.

Granny tables are seen in most home fashion magazines that feature Early American furniture. The ads say that Granny had to use a nail keg or a pickle barrel to do what you can do with these inexpensive, yet sturdy tables. They can be used as end tables, utility tables, candle stands, or TV snack tables to mention just a few.

Dimensions vary and they can be built to suit the particular use you have in mind. The tops vary from 20 inches to 42 inches. The larger tables can even be used in a breakfast nook or small kitchen.

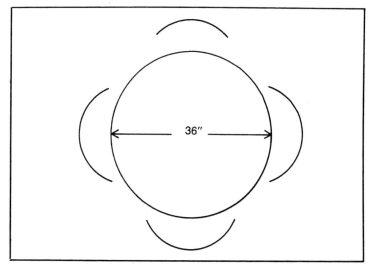

Fig. 12-3. Table for Four (Round).

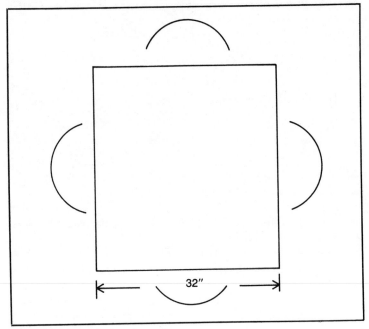

Fig. 12-4. Table for Four (Square).

The smallest table (Fig. 12-8) with a 20-inch top has three legs. The legs can vary from 18 inches to 26 inches high, depending on your taste and needs. All the rest have four legs for stability.

Here are some of Granny's own dimensions. The tops that have a 24-inch, 30-inch, 36-inch, or 42-inch top are all 27 inches high.

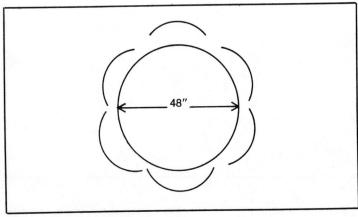

Fig. 12-5. Table for Six (Round).

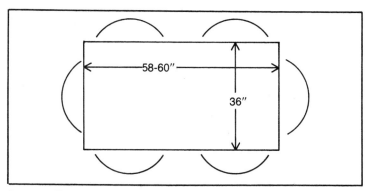

Fig. 12-6. Table for Six (Rectangular).

Because Granny was partial to round tops—she was used to hitting the pickle barrel—any variation of the round top is your perogative. But it looses its authenticity as a Granny table. Who knows, you might invent an Uncle Zek table.

Granny tables were not necessarily free-form furniture. Probably none were. To adapt the table to a free edge style, just cut a 1½″ or 2″ thick cross slice from a log about 20″ wide (or whatever width you want) and put legs on it. See Fig. 12-9.

It would even look good with a set of those commercial legs that you can buy and attach with the brackets provided. Stain them to match the top and complete with the finish of your choice. Granny would probably like you to paint it white, but then Granny usually

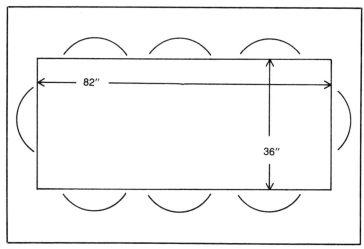

Fig. 12-7. A table for eight.

Fig. 12-8. This table is actually an unfinished sign. The story is that a friend of mine built a house and named it "Tir Tairngiri." That is a Gaelic phrase attributed to St. Brenden and meaning something like "Place of Fulfillment". Before I got to the large ornate "K" at the bottom, I found out he changed the name of the newly constructed home to "Ballycoyne." He dropped the Kil (meaning "illegitimate son of"). So I made the sign into a table. The wood is cherry. The finish is a high gloss polyurethane. And I won't give it to him.

Fig. 12-9. A granny table (in free-form style) and a granny table covered with topper (or possibly a pickle board covered with a topper).

put a "topper" over it. That is a fabric cover that hung to the floor. If you are going to do that, you might as well use the pickle barrel to start with and save yourself some work.

Chapter 13

Stools

A bar stool is usually about 30 inches high and has a 14-inch seat. If there is a footrest, it should be about 8 inches off the floor. A back is optional. See Fig. 13-1.

A kitchen stool should be about 23 to 25 inches high with a 12-inch to 14-inch seat.

A stool for a drafting table will be about 26 inches high with a 14-inch seat.

Short stools are 17 to 18 inches high and they have a 14-inch to 15-inch seat. See Fig. 13-2.

Here is a one-evening project that can be very useful and bring its share of comments. This stool is 20″ long, 11½″ wide and 12″ high. It is made from ⅝″ stock with the free edge on both sides. Cut the top from a board close to a foot wide. Cut the legs from a slightly narrower board. These legs are 10½″ wide. Make them about 11½″ long (11⅜″ if you want the stool exactly 12″). If you want the design in the bottom of the legs, come in 2″ from each side and 1½″ from the bottom. Draw your lines and round the corner. See Figure 13-2. Cut with a jig or sabre saw. The stringer, or support between the legs, will be 14¾″ that will position the legs 2 inches in from the ends of the stool. It should be about 4″ wide. The free ridge should go on the bottom. After you have all the pieces cut out, sand them completely.

First, the bevel on the top piece should face up (the more narrow side up). On the legs the bevel should face out. The easiest way to attach the legs to the top is to put a glue block on the inside of

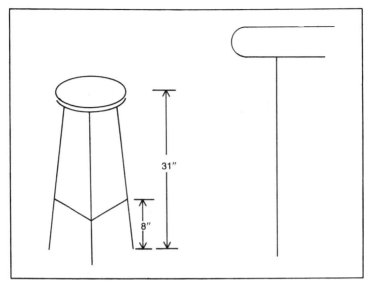

Fig. 13-1. A barstool design.

each leg and both glue and screw it to the underside of the top and the leg. Make the glue block from 1"-×-1" stock about 8½" long. You can put the screws into the block and through to the leg or top, but a stronger joint will be obtained by putting the screws through the top into the block and through the outside of the legs to the block. These can be countersunk and plugged with dowels. The stringer should be attached with glue and screws in the same manner as above; screws are countersunk and through the leg into the stringer. Place the

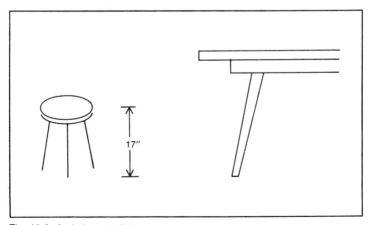

Fig. 13-2. A chair stool design.

Fig. 13-3. A utility stool.

bottom of the stringer about 2½" above the notch you cut out of the leg. That puts the stringer about 4" off the floor. So there you have it. Leave it natural or stain and finish it to match the decor. And don't be afraid to put your feet on it. I even use mine as an ottoman when my favorite cinder block is not handy. See Fig. 13-3.

Chapter 14

Beds

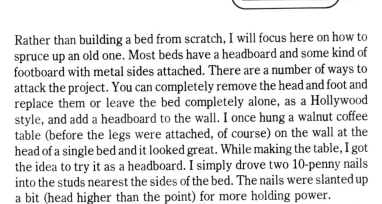

Rather than building a bed from scratch, I will focus here on how to spruce up an old one. Most beds have a headboard and some kind of footboard with metal sides attached. There are a number of ways to attack the project. You can completely remove the head and foot and replace them or leave the bed completely alone, as a Hollywood style, and add a headboard to the wall. I once hung a walnut coffee table (before the legs were attached, of course) on the wall at the head of a single bed and it looked great. While making the table, I got the idea to try it as a headboard. I simply drove two 10-penny nails into the studs nearest the sides of the bed. The nails were slanted up a bit (head higher than the point) for more holding power.

I drilled two ½" holes in the back of the table at the same angle, hung it on the nails and, bang—the job was finished in less than half an hour. Just make sure that the nails are level and that the holes match. It is a simple job of measuring accurately.

If you would rather position the board as a shelf, you can put it on legs or attach it to the wall with wooden or metal brackets. It could be at mattress level and end at the sides of the bed or extend beyond them as night tables.

This provides a nice way of transforming the look of your whole bedroom by just finishing one board (Fig. 14-1). The idea can be adapted to a double bed with one long board or twin beds using either one long or two shorter pieces. Either configuration works and the height of the shelf-type headboard can be adjusted to suit your taste.

Fig. 14-1. A shelf used instead of a headboard.

This headboard can be raised a foot or 18 inches above the bed and mounted as a shelf or positioned with a backing board. See 14-2.

With any type of headboard, you are free to add sides and a foot to the bed. You could easily convert it to "Hollywood" style or copy the dimensions somewhat from the original. See Fig. 14-3.

If you do add these pieces, butt them in using one of the techniques discussed for adding sides and kickboards to a chair or couch.

Many times the sides are nothing more than metal angle irons. These can be drilled and the side board can be screwed in place for the inside of the angle. A screw every 2 feet should do it. Joining it to the head and footboard will keep it from wobbling on you.

The footboard will present more of a challenge. If there is an existing board to be removed, it might be the sole support of the sides. In most cases, this will be the situation. It is easily removed, but the new footboard will then have to be equipped with casters.

When you screw the side angle irons into the new foot, be sure you have them level and the same distance from the floor that they were when you took them off. Placing the casters on is not a big problem. If your footboard is wide enough, 1½ to 2 inches, you can drill a hole in the bottom and stick in the casters.

100

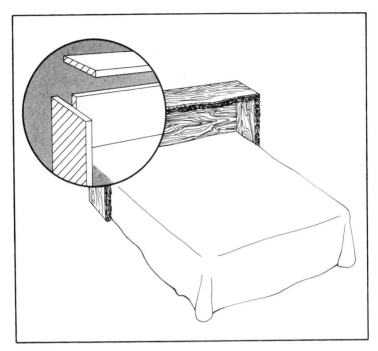

Fig. 14-2. A shelf-type headboard.

I prefer them somewhat recessed under the bed. In this case, just add a piece of 2 × 4 on the inside of the footboard just inside the spot you will fasten the angle irons and low enough that the wood

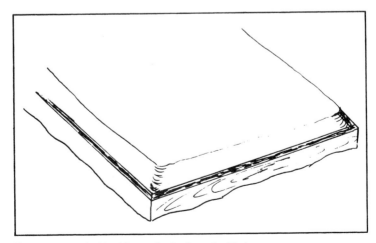

Fig. 14-3. A bed with sides and a footboard added.

will not interfere with the bottom of the box spring. In other words, make sure that the top of the legs do not come above the bottom of the angle irons. Drill the 2 × 4 and position the casters as usual. The same system applies to the headboard.

Before you start, examine the bed and figure out how much you want to do and the method you want to use (butt the joints, mitered joints, etc.). Whether you put the sides or the head and foot on first is a matter of choice. I usually do the sides first. When they are pulled in tight to the angle irons and positioned the proper distance apart, you have a good measurement for your footboard.

Mitered joints must be cut exactly. Butted joints are easier. In this case, cut the sides about 1/16 over on each end. Have this extend beyond the flat part of the bracket that you will attach to the footboard. This will allow you to pull the board in tight and make a good joint. Butt the footboard against the ends of the side boards. Cut this a hair long and later you can sand it flush with a belt sander.

Finish sanding to a satin smoothness. Apply a finish and postpone your nap until it dries.

Chapter 15

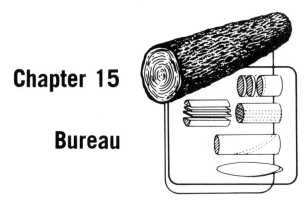

Bureau

To some, this chapter might seem overly simple and short for such a big job as making a bureau to match your newly created bed. Because the scope of this project is to recover an existing bureau with wood, it really is not that difficult. This way you can avoid the sometimes difficult task of making drawers and having them fit and slide properly. This method will not work on pieces with curved drawers or sides.

Choose a bureau with straight lines and drawers that work or can be made to work easily. Tighten all loose joints with glue and screws. Don't worry if the screws show, but countersink them just a hair so that they will not interfere with your cover boards. Remove or reglue all loose veneer. Take the drawers out and remove all knobs or handles. Sand around the holes and remove any high spots. With a medium-weight sandpaper, rough up the face of the drawers, top, and sides, removing all loose paint or varnish. There is no need to remove the entire finish. This sanding is mainly to provide a better bonding surface for glue.

The top of the old bureau might give you some moments of extra thought. Most bureaus have the top extending beyond the sides and drawers, and most have some sort of rounded edges or decorative-routed edges. These will definitely interfere with your overall plan. You have two choices for an easy solution. Remove the top and proceed without it or cut the edges off flush all the way around. If you can get the top off, I suggest that method. After you have removed it, sand off all the dried glue.

You are now ready to go. I suggest that you use a stock no thicker than 1 inch. You could do so if you are after a very heavy-looking bureau. Most bureaus are about 18 inches deep. I hope that your boards are that wide or wider so that you will not have to piece them together.

Start with the sides first. Cut your board flush with the top, bottom, and front of your existing side. You will have to cut the free-edge square on the front, but you could have it on the back side and bottom if you prefer. In cutting a free-edge square, I prefer to cut off as little as possible so that I still retain some of the varying tones of the sapwood. How much you take off the board will be determined by its natural width.

If you want to have the free edge on the back, make sure all of the side is covered and that the floating edge extends beyond the back edge of the side. Then mark the front edge and cut it flush. Attach the new sides to the existing sides with a good wood glue (follow the manufacturer's directions).

Fasten with screws from inside the bureau through the support frame and the old sides into the new board. Secure on all four sides about every 18 inches and here and there through the side itself, (if it is thick enough to hold a screw), in the pattern of X or +. You may have to countersink these screws so that they will not interfere with the movement of the drawers.

Take the piece you intend to use for the front (drawer section). I suggest that you take these from one board in order to get a matched grain rather than use scraps. See Figure 15-1. What you are aiming for here is to have the new drawer fronts butt against one another. They might be that way on your existing piece or they might fit into the frame with about an inch separating each drawer. Neither will present a problem.

If all the drawers butt, cut each drawer from the piece to the exact size of the original face. Do each drawer in sequence (working up or down) from the same end of the board. Try to make each cut square so that the sides will be square and the grain will be straight. This also will avoid interrupting the matching grain by trimming the board square between drawers. If the existing drawers fit into the frame and are separated by it, add that distance to the top of each drawer front. Start at the top so that all spaces are covered by the new fronts. You can even juggle these from one drawer to another in order to make the drawer fronts more equal or to make them larger or smaller to break up the symmetry.

For example, if you have four drawers with three spacers

between them (one at the top, one at the bottom), you can cover the top spacer and one below it with the face of the top drawer. With the face of the bottom drawer, the bottom spacer and the one above it can be covered. This leaves you one spacer in the middle and two drawers. Cover the spacer completely with one drawer or split the distance between the bottom and top of drawers two and three. See Fig. 15-2.

Now that you have all the drawers cut out and numbered on the reverse side to keep them in the proper order, attach them to the existing fronts of the drawers. Use glue and screws.

I usually drill six holes in each drawer face before I apply the glue. Drill them from the inside of the drawer because this will show you if you have to drill them on an angle to make room for the bulky drill. You could use a small, hand-ratchet drill and avoid that problem. I don't because I don't own one.

If your face wood is pine or poplar, you do not have to continue the pilot holes into the new piece. If it is oak or walnut, this will be a must or you will never get the screws into it.

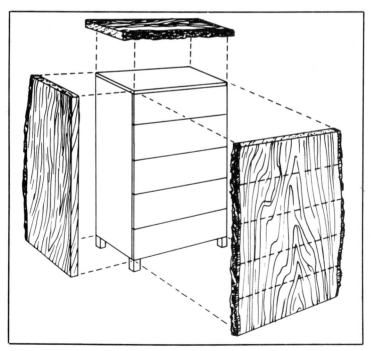

Fig. 15-1. One full board is used to make the drawers in order to maintain the grain.

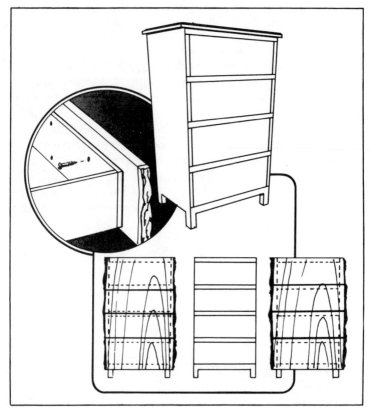

Fig. 15-2. Ways to use facing boards on drawers.

Once the holes are in the drawer front, glue both pieces. Position them carefully in place and clamp them. I clamp the whole thing to the work bench. This gets the one end of the clamps out of the way and you have a good solid surface to apply pressure to the screws. Run the pilot holes part way into the new wood and screw tightly.

Now you are ready for the top. The top should hang over the sides and front a bit. How much is your choice. Anything from ¼ inch to about 1 inch is acceptable. If you come up with an unusual design and if you like it, do it. Cut the top to size, flush in the back, position it, glue it, and fasten it with screws from the inside. Finish it to your taste. If the legs do not match, replace them or sand them and stain to match.

You'll probably lose some sleep admiring your new bedroom furniture!

Chapter 16

Table Lamps

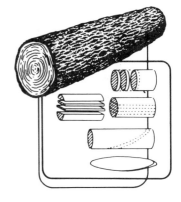

Having considered the larger pieces used in a home, let's examine some of the smaller appointments that finish off a room and carry the free form theme throughout. Good taste dictates that you don't clutter up the place by overdoing it. But your taste might also dictate that you replace a modern lamp, of chrome and smoke plastic, in a room with natural wood furniture. In our modern and somewhat confusing times you can mix almost anything and often get away with it. Because I have an aversion to much mixing of styles, I have included in this chapter some economical and easily made replacements.

First look at the table lamp. I think that a piece of driftwood mixes quite well with free-form furniture. I discovered this quite by accident. In my room, on the free-form table next to a lounge chair, was a lamp that I had fashioned from an unusual wine bottle. At a party one evening, an over-indulgent friend knocked it off the table and smashed it beyond repair.

Desperately needing a replacement to place near my favorite chair—and being pressed for time due to teaching in a high school, a college, marking papers, preparing classes, writing this book, all coupled with other duties and demands on my time, plus a growing aversion to buying ready-made things—I looked for the fastest and least expensive way out of my lamp problem. Salvaging the usable parts from the broken lamp—the shade assembly, socket, pipe, and cord—I descended to the workshop to inventory what I had available to make a lamp. My eye caught a piece of driftwood.

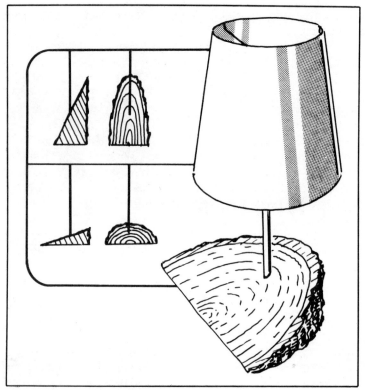

Fig. 16-1. The tall and flat wedge shapes for a lamp base. Any height and angle between these is perfectly acceptable.

I didn't care if it fit in with the decor or not, I needed a lamp. I drilled a hole in the driftwood the size of the pipe, added white glue, hammered it in, ran the cord, put the top on, varnished the driftwood, and took it to my room. Within a half hour, I had a new lamp that I liked. As a matter of fact, I love it.

Here are a few thoughts on driftwood. If the base is too big it will look awkward. You don't want the base to take up the whole table. Some people like driftwood unfinished. Some like it with a satin finish or a high gloss. Driftwood looks more rustic if you apply a wood bleach. This makes the wood a grayish weather-beaten color. Take your choice. You might want to match whatever finish you have on your furniture and see how you like it. Remember that once you varnish driftwood you can't bleach it.

When cutting down small trees, 8 to 15 inches in diameter, I always save the wedge cut. I have made innumerable lamps from oak, cherry, walnut, maple, ash, pine, and even a moth-eaten apple and pear tree.

The wedge lamp is relatively easy. Position the wedge with whatever side up that looks best to you. See Figs. 16-1 through 16-3. About one-quarter of the way down the face from the top, drill through completely and come out the bottom. A long drill bit might follow the crooked grain lines and curve some on you. It doesn't matter where you come out as long as it is on the bottom and not on the sides. Usually you can keep the first few inches of your hole with the shorter, stronger bit. It should give you the couple inches of true, straight hole that you need. You have the option then of drilling in the back about an inch from the bottom and trying to meet the other hole. Use a slightly larger bit for this. Occasionally you will be lucky and hit it on the first try.

In attempting to fish the wire through the hole, around the right angle and up the shaft, use a piece of thin wire first. Push it through and then pull the cord through. If the cord is not too thick, you will have no trouble. If you want the cord on the bottom, make a slot for it. It is much easier to use a router or a series of small holes drilled about ½ inch deep into the bottom toward the back of the base and straightened with a chisel. The cord is stapled in this slot and it

Fig. 16-2. Oak wedge used as base for lamp on a night table. Notice that the shade on this lamp is too small for the height of the stem.

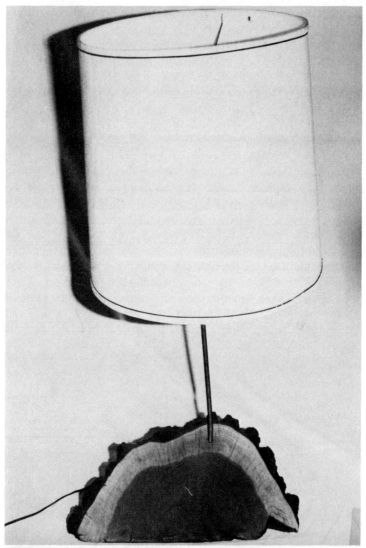

Fig. 16-3. Walnut wedge. Notice that the pipe is not placed directly in the center of the wedge.

allows the lamp to conceal the cord and sit firmly. Take extreme caution not to pierce the cord with a staple or you will cause a fire hazard, possibly burn your house, and all your hard work and creativity will go up in smoke.

Before inserting the cord, have the piece completely sanded.

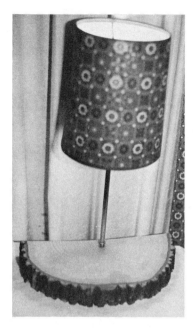

Fig. 16-4. A cross cut of ash was cut in half and used as a base for a night lamp.

Leave the varnishing (or whatever finish you prefer) to last. It will get scratched during the drilling and jostling around that you give it. Before you insert the pipe, fish the wire through *almost* to the top of the pipe. Then hammer or screw the pipe into the wood (putting

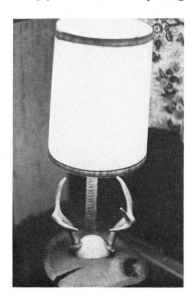

Fig. 16-5. A cross cut of cherry complete with a crack and a rotten spot is a very acceptable base. The pipe was wound with clothesline and stained. The antlers are merely setting on the base; they are not part of the lamp. This particular base is too small to have anything so busy as that on it.

111

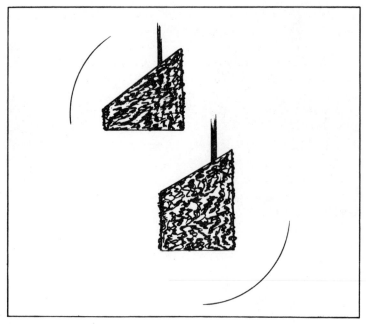

Fig. 16-6. Examples of the variation of the wedge shape. These are a much heavier and rustic looking lamp. These are nice when you have a wood such as cherry or pear. Remove the back and show off the wood.

glue into the hole also). If you use a hammer, hold a piece of 2 × 4 on top of the pipe so that you don't bugger up the threads that hold the socket. Also be sure not to pinch the wire between the pipe and the wood. Keep the wire taut. Push the wire up, put the socket on, and connect the socket. Let the glue dry 24 hours, touch up the sanding, and apply a finish.

If your pipe is exactly what you want that's fine, but if you used an old pipe of the wrong color or the commercial type that is threaded all the way down you may find it unacceptable. You can doctor it up in a number of ways. A plain copper pipe can be brightened with fine steel wool and sprayed with a commercial spray can of lacquer or an artist fixative to keep it bright. You can spray it with black or bronze paint or any color that will pick up the scheme of a room.

I have also wrapped pipe with a rope clothes line. Some look good left white or sprayed with lacquer or fixative to keep it clean; others I stained walnut or oak or whatever. A dark rope can be lacquered if you prefer. A friend of mine fixed small sea shells up the pipe to hide the unsightly condition of it. It's OK if you like sea shells. I prefer a copper pipe that retains its original color or a piece of copper tubing over an ugly pipe.

Other lamp bases you could use are the cross or diagonal slice of a tree. Thickness depends on preference. One or 2 inches for the diagonal cut is fine and you can have up to 12 or 14 inches for the

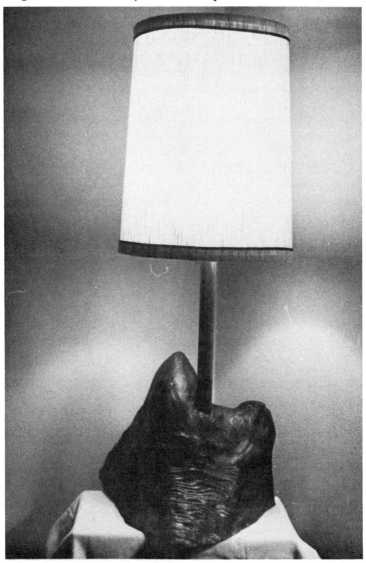

Fig. 16-7. This is a piece of walnut. The section was cut from the root of a large tree. A piece of copper tubing was used for the pipe.

cross-cut. For pieces that are not very thick, make sure the base is wide enough to support the weight of the socket and shade without becoming unsteady. See Fig. 16-4 and 16-5.

Another variation is the log that is cut off on a diagonal on the top and has a bottom flat. See Fig. 16-6. Make the bottom cut square with the log and the top cut on an angle. This method exposes the grain and makes a more decorative piece. On all these, you can glue a piece of felt, on the bottom so as not to scratch the table.

For a finishing touch, top off your new lamp with a lampshade that fits. The dimensions of shades vary as to width and depth. If the shade looks out of place try another style. The shade can be decorated to your taste. I have used wallpaper or various labels and wallpaper paste to fix them to a plain lampshade. You might wish to decoupage your favorite picture or photo on the shade.

Many other novel shapes can be made into table lamps. An off-shaped piece you have might take on possibilities after you study it for awhile. See Fig. 16-7.

Chapter 17

Clocks

Another interesting appointment is the wall clock. Any piece of wood from ½" to a couple of inches thick can be used. Round or diagonal slices usually make very attractive clocks because of the grain effect. See Fig. 17-1.

Even pieces of wood with a rotted section can be used to obtain a rather unusual effect. Dig out the rot and do not fill the hole. See Fig. 17-2.

A diagonal cut from an irregular log produces varied shapes that sometimes cannot be duplicated. See Figs. 17-3 and 17-4.

Even a square or rectangular piece of board can be used with pleasing effects. See Figs. 17-5 and 17-6.

I once had all the boards from a walnut tree split and broken in half lengthwise as they went through the blade at the sawmill. Some trees have a stress point and you have no way of knowing about it until it is cut. If a board is cut in such a way that the stress runs through the plank, it breaks and explodes down the stress line. Fortunately this is not too common. It was my dumb luck to cut the log perfectly perpendicular to the stress.

Being stuck with half boards that I had paid to have cut was very distressing. From these I invented my own style of desk clock. See Fig. 17-7. Cut off a piece about 6" square. You can leave the bark on or off and have it on the top or side. Cut the bottom on a slight bevel so the clock will lean back slightly. You will have to glue a small block on the back to keep it steady. Draw an X on the *front,* not the back, to find center. Drill a ½" hole all the way through. Place

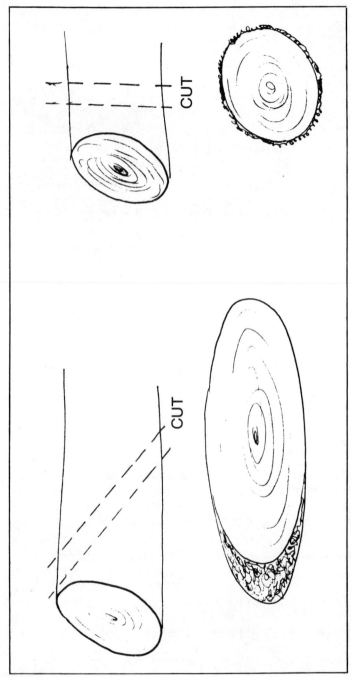

Fig. 17-1. An example of a diagonal cross-sectional cut.

Fig. 17-2. An example of wood with a rotted section.

the battery-powered clock mechanism on the back with the shaft in the newly drilled hole and draw a line around the case.

This is the area you will have to dig out if the wood is more than ½″ thick. There are a few methods for doing this. Using a router is the easiest. If you do not have a router, you can drill a few holes with a 1″ expansion bit. If you don't have one of these, you will have to drill 20 or 30 holes close together with a ½″ bit. I know you have that because you used it to drill the center hole. Clean out the area with a chisel.

You want to get to within ½″ of the face or whatever will allow the shaft of the mechanism to extend out enough to get the face nut

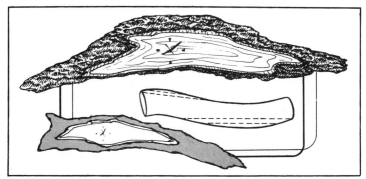

Fig. 17-3. A cross-sectional cut.

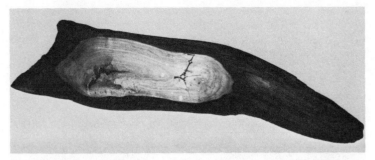

Fig. 17-4. A cross-section cut.

on it. The inside of your hole need only be relatively smooth. Sand and apply a finish. Insert the mechanism, tighten the lock nut and install the hands. If you remembered to buy a battery, you now have a working desk clock. The clock works can be purchased at most hobby and craft shops.

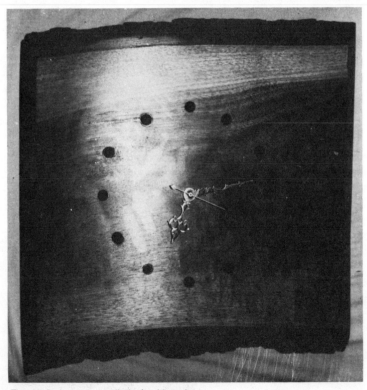

Fig. 17-5. A square wall clock with walnut.

Fig. 17-6. A square wall clock (bark on top only) with walnut.

In order to use up my split wood, I made these clocks for Christmas gifts and wedding gifts. I saved a pile of money and I was able to give something that I thought would be appreciated more because of the personal touch.

Fig. 17-7. A desk clock (walnut).

Chapter 18

Accessories

A nice little touch to personalize a room is a stand-up ashtray. The easiest way to "free form" it is simply to take an existing ashtray and remove the base and top. Replace the stems with a 2-inch or 3-inch piece of log the same length as the stem you took out. See Fig. 18-1.

Cut the stem to size. Make sure that the cuts are square or the thing will lean when finished. Strip the bark if you like and apply a finish. I always use the same wood I used for the rest of the furniture in the room, and I also finish it the same way.

When you take an ashtray apart, you will probably find a rod, all way through, threaded on both ends with a nut at the top and bottom holding it all together. It would be too much trouble and also unnecessary to drill through your log and replace the pipe. Instead attach the top and base with long, flat-head wood screws. Drill a pilot hole in the stem with a bit a little smaller than the screw. Scrape the screw a few times across a bar of soap before screwing it in. This will make it easier to tighten. If it is too hard to turn it all the way down, redrill the pilot hole with the next size larger drill.

Save the rod you took out of the center. If it is not solid, you might be able to use it to make a lamp.

If the base of the ash tray is not satisfactory—too ornate or too beat up—you could replace it with wood. Your taste and what is available will determine what style of base you use. You might prefer a 1- or 2-inch thick cross section of a 10- or 12-inch log. See Fig. 18-2.

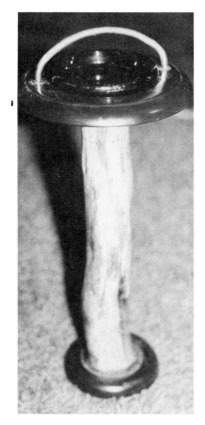

Fig. 18-1. An oak log was used as the stem for this ashtray. The top and bottom were painted black.

Fig. 18-2. A cross section of a log used for the base of an ashtray.

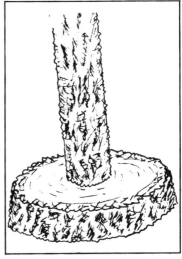

You could use a piece of scrap from another piece of furniture and fashion that into a base, or even a base and center post. See Fig. 18-3. Attach the parts in the same manner as above (with long, wood screws).

If you prefer making the complete stand from wood, you will be getting into the problem of digging out or routing out the top so that an ashtray will sit snugly. If you have the tools, time and patience, go to it. But it is much easier to use the standard top. Spray paint it if you must.

If you still would rather have a free-form top, the best bet is to use a round piece about 2½ or 3 inches thick and dig out the center to the depth of the ashtray that you are going to use. This can be done with a hammer and chisel or router. If you use the hammer, chisel, and chop method, first drill some holes in the wood; it makes it easier to dig out. Don't drill too deeply. Finish the entire piece to match the existing wood.

Fig. 18-3. The base and stem were fashioned out of pine to match the furniture.

COAT RACK

There are other appointments that you can sprinkle throughout your home. One of my favorites is the coat rack. I purchased a coat rack at a garage sale because I liked the hooks, but not the backing board. I removed the hooks and polished them. Lo and behold they were brass. I used the back for firewood. I cut a 3-foot section from a walnut slab I had that was about 6″ wide. The brass on the dark walnut was very striking.

A friend of mine had four deer hooves prepared by a taxidermist. He asked me for a backing board. I used an 8-inch wide piece of walnut because the hooves were heavier looking than my brass hooks. It turned out to be a beautiful combination of dead tree and dead deer.

If you don't have brass hooks—like the ones I practically stole at that garage sale—or deer hooves, you can use plain dowels for the hooks. Use four for a 3-foot board and have them angle slightly upward. Exactly how much of an angle you use will be according to your taste. Make the dowel extend out about 3 inches and use ½-inch stock dowel for a 6-inch wide board and ⅝-inch dowel for 8-inch board.

Plant the dowel deep enough to support the weight of a coat. I usually drill to within ⅛ inch of going all the way through the backing board. Glue the dowel well. Score the dowel, as previously explained, but only on the part that will be buried in the wood. Stain the dowels as close to the shade of the backing board as possible. It should look quite acceptable, but keep your eye out for brass at the next garage sale you attend.

SCONCE

I have found that a sconce is a very easy accessory to make and, at least for my own taste, it is one of those small yet rich touches that an area might need. The variations of design are unlimited. The easiest is a diagonal slice of about 8 or 9 inches wide, about 14 inches high, and 1 inch thick. You could even make the sconce and clock from the same log for a matching set.

From the basic diagonal slice design, you are free to take off in many directions. One of the nicest designs I have done resulted when I took the candle holder off an all-brass sconce and attached just the holder part to the free-form back. See Fig. 18-4.

How you will attach the candle holder to the free form depends on how the holder is made. If there are threads on the end, you can

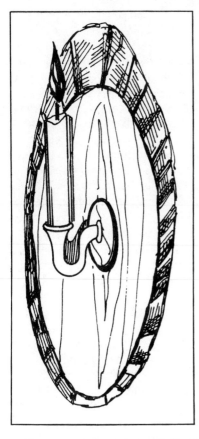

Fig. 18-4. A brass candle holder on a diagonal cut from a log.

drill a hole that is slightly *smaller* than the rod or threaded pipe and just screw it into the wood. Add some glue to this process and it may be a tight enough fit to hold steady. If not, then you might have to countersink a nut in the back of the wood and screw the holder into the nut for support.

Countersink the nut about ½ or ⅝ of an inch if the threads are long enough to reach. If you have to sink the nut any deeper, you are making the wall between the nut and the face of the sconce dangerously thin. It could crack if you tighten the holder on the nut just a bit too hard. In most cases though, the wood will hold. If the holder has no threads to start with, your only recourse is to glue the thing into a snug hold in the wood. I like this sconce the best of any I have made or seen. I think the marriage of natural wood and brass tends to have a touch of elegance.

If a brass, silver, or iron candle holder is not available, you can make one from wood. I prefer not overcrowding the sconce with free-form edges and I make the candle holder part from cut wood with no free edge on it.

Fasten the candle holder with one or two screws inserted through the back of the plaque into the holder through drilled pilot holes. See Fig. 18-5. If your preference is to carry the "free edge" theme to the holder, you could take a cross-section slice of a limb, about 4 inches in diameter, and cut yourself a piece about ¾ off about an inch thick. Cut this in half along the diagonal. See Fig. 18-6.

Drill a hole the size you need for the candle you have in mind. Attach this candle base with two screws inserted from the back of the plaque into the base through drilled pilot holes. This is another type of sconce that can be of some interest or better fit your decor.

You might want to vary the style somewhat, but here's how the sconce shown in Fig. 18-7 was made. Choose a piece of branch or limb roughly 4 inches in diameter. Your choice of wood should take into consideration the grain effect if you are not already locked into the use of a specific wood to match something. The sconce shown in Fig. 18-7 is walnut.

First choose which side of the log you want for the back and front. Very little of the front will be left after you cut it, but make

Fig. 18-5. An idea for a shape to use when making a candle holder from wood.

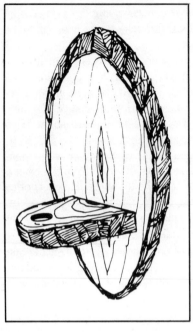

Fig. 18-6. A candle holder from a cross-cut log.

sure the part that remains is not chipped or marred in any way. If there is a flat piece to the log, I like to use it in the back. Secure the log in a vise with two buffer boards. Cut the level in the top and bottom. You could put the log in a mitre box—laying on its side—and cut the levels on a 45° angle.

Make sure that the levels are facing the front. Do not have them cocked in different directions. The angle of each cut need not be the same. What you are after is to show some grain at the top and bottom and break up dull 90° angles.

Next, mark the center of the log and draw a line, square with your level for your cut, down the length of the piece. Decide how far down you want to cut and mark the spot that will be squared off for the candle holder. Chalk is a good marker, especially if the bark is still on the wood.

When you make these cuts be *very* careful that you do not cut beyond the point where the two saw cuts meet. Cut each one almost to this intersection and finish them alternately, little by little, so that they exactly meet.

If you go too far on either cut—or worse, on both cuts—you will have a line at the base of your holder and it will look sloppy. For making these cuts, you can use a sharp handsaw, a saber saw, or whatever combination is easiest. I have even used a chain saw when I had a heavy-duty disc sander available to make the rest of the job easy. When you have made your cuts, start your sanding, sanding, and sanding. Drill a hole in the platform the size you need to accommodate the candle you have in mind.

Your choice might be for a more plain design. See Fig. 18-8. The cutting is easier and, as I have tried to emphasize, there is a certain beauty in simplicity. The simplest way to hang these things on a wall is to drill a ½ inch hole in the back of the sconce and hang it on a nail. Simple? Well maybe! You might put the hole in the center and still find the sconce hangs crookedly. This could happen because the density of the wood on one side of the limb is greater than on the other. You can hammer a small nail into the back and hang the sconce on the edge of your work bench to see if it hangs straight.

Move the nail slightly until the sconce hangs properly and then drill a hole in that spot. Angle the hole slightly up. Be careful not to go so deep that you come out the other side. If you have two sconces, be sure to put both holes the same distance from the top so that they hang evenly.

SIGNS

People are unpredictable. Sometimes they heap well-deserved

Fig. 18-7. A walnut sconce cut from a log.

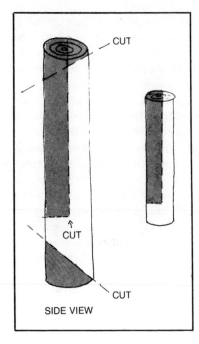

Fig. 18-8. The side view of a sconce made from a log. Dotted lines show cuts.

CUT

CUT

CUT

SIDE VIEW

praise on the creator of beautiful free-form furniture. Others will enter the same room and never notice it. The most incredible person is the well-meaning visitor who stands in the middle of your labors and creative endeavors, takes it all in, and comments pro-fusely only on some insignificant afterthought you whipped up and threw in. This has happened to me a number of times.

I have an entirely furnished room that contains a couch, a chair, four tables, two lamps, and two clocks of deep, thick, free-form cherry—and a sign. I had a cross-cut of cherry log, 14″ in diameter, 2″ thick, and deemed it too small for the table I needed.

I had it completely sanded and wanted to seal it to help keep it from cracking. I had nothing in mind that I wanted to use it for. For the want of something else to do with the piece, I decided to make a sign of some sort. I had already made name and address signs for all my friends. I looked through a mail-order catalog to find a catchy saying or design. "Shalom" leapt out so I copied it onto the wood, routed it out, applied a finish, and hung it in my room. I love it; it gives me great personal satisfaction at having done it. In other ways it has constantly militated against my mild ego trips. People tend to ignore what I consider my greatest accomplishments (couch and furniture) and notice nothing but that little sign.

Fortunately, personal satisfaction is sufficient. The praise is nice, but I wouldn't part with my "Shalom" even though it does steal the limelight. Something such as this offers an added personal touch that tends to incorporate itself onto the personality of the room.

Out of what can you make a sign? Just about anything. Most have some kind of flat surface. A cross cut, a diagonal cut or a slab will work. All of the illustrations of clocks in this chapter show styles of wood that could have been made into signs instead. A name or an address number can be used for a sign hung outside. For inside use, a name or initial can be placed over a fireplace or in a den. They are perfect for wall plaques to decorate an unadorned wall.

Sand the wood to a fine finish. Draw or trace your letters, numbers, or design on the smooth surface. Now you have the option of painting the figures or digging them with a router, or even burning them in with a wood-burning pencil. Painting is the easiest method.

You can use one tone that contrasts with the wood or a multi-colored configuration or picture. At any rate, when your paint is well dried or the wood-burning is finished, you are ready to apply the varnish, lacquer, polyurethane or other finish. The finishes usually go over the paint with no problem and it will not disturb it. It is always a good idea to put a few dashes of the paint you are using on a test piece of wood or even on the back of your sign. First try your finish over that particular paint and make sure that it will not lift it and ruin your whole project.

If you dig out your letters or designs with a router, it would   a good idea to apply a dark stain or paint to the letters in order to set up a contrast with the tone of the wood. Cover both the bottom and sides of the dug out part. Let this dry completely. Then sand the top again with fine paper so that you clean up the edges of the letters in case your stain or paint seeped out over the sides. Blow all the sanding dust out of the letters before you apply the finish.

Photos and illustrations give just a few ideas of what can be done with signs. One of the more memorable signs I have done was a coat of arms on a large cross-cut of walnut. Still the name and address is the most popular. One variation of this I saw was a sign that read: House of So and So. Underneath the names was 1976. The date is the year the couple was married. I don't know who thought of the idea, but on a free-form sign with Old English Lettering, it lends a touch of class to a plain old name sign.

Another personal twist that I like is to use the name in its original language. With names that have been anglicized from any

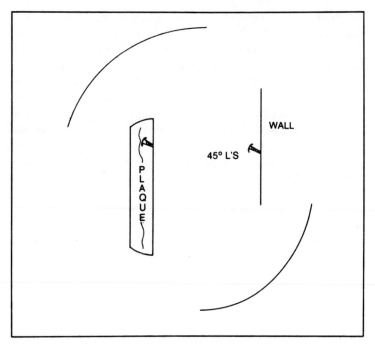

Fig. 18-9. How to drill and hang a sign on a plaque.

language that has a different alphabet than our own, it is interesting to add the surname in the original characters. Examples of this would be Greek, Hebrew, or Chinese. If you like an idea, try it. You may hit on a real conversation piece.

How to Hang Signs

If your sign is to go on a wall, it is relatively easy to hang it. The bottom line is that you put a hole in the back of the sign and a nail in the wall and hang it. When you put the nail in the wall, make sure you first find the joist and then nail into it. Use about an 8-penny finishing nail and put it in at a 45° angle. Let about 1 inch of the nail extend out.

Use a ½" bit and drill into the back of the sign about 4" down from the top. Angle your bit about 45° up. See Fig. 18-9.

Post Construction

If you hang your sign outside, you might have to construct a post assembly. If possible, use 4 × 4 posts of cedar or redwood. If they are not available, use as hard a wood as you can and put creosote on the section below ground and wood preserver on the section above ground.

If you use paint, dark brown is probably the most common color used. Use any color to match your house or fence.

Choose your vertical post, long enough so that you can bury 2 to 3 feet in the ground and still have 54″ of post exposed. If your sign is light, 2 feet should be enough to anchor it in the ground. If you have a heavy sign or an exceptionally windy location, bury the post in some cement to a depth of 3 feet.

Length

Assuming you will bury your post 36″ in the ground and have it 54″ high, Cut your 4 × 4 post 90″ long. Your cross number will be exactly 36″ long.

You might want to put a chamfer on all four sides of each post. This should be only ¼″ in on each face and then be planed smooth. Or you might prefer to sand the sharp end to a gentle round. No matter which way you go with the long sides, you do want to chamfer the ends of each piece. Chamfer the butt end of the top of the vertical post and both ends of the horizontal one. See Fig. 18-10.

Measure at least ⅜″ in from the ends of the board and draw a line all the way around. Now measure the same distance on the open end grain for all four sides. Draw lines. Plane or saw off the waste between the lines.

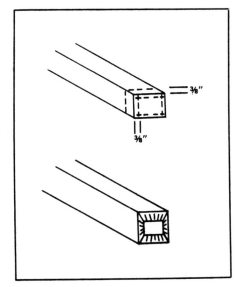

Fig. 18-10. A chamfer.

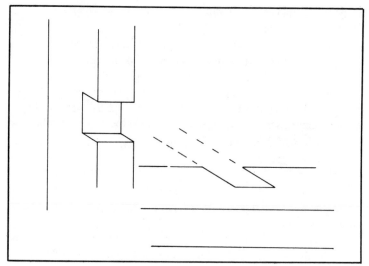

Fig. 18-11. A notch in a vertical post. The same notch is cut in a horizontal post.

Notching

You will want to notch the two posts so that they will be stronger and make a neater joint. See Fig. 18-11. Measure from the top end of vertical post 6″ and draw a line. Do this on three sides. If your posts are a true 4″, measure another 4″ from your line and draw another line. Do this on the same three sides. Or measure the exact width and measure this distance instead of the 4″ mentioned. See Fig. 18-12.

On the middle side between the lines you drew, draw diagonal lines or blacken it with a pencil. On the two adjacent sides, again between the lines you draw, draw a line *exactly* one-half the width of the post. See Fig. 18-13.

Now consider the horizontal piece. Do exactly the same as you did on the vertical piece. Measure 6″ and draw a line on 3 sides. Measure 4″ farther in, or the width of your post, and draw a line on the same three sides. Black out the middle side and draw the lines one-half the width on the adjacent sides.

In order to cut out the section on each post, set your saw blade as deep as you need the cut (one-half the width) and cut slightly on the inside of the lines you drew. Make several cuts between the lines. Chisel out the waste. The notches fit together and are held by two 4″ long carriage bolts. See Fig. 18-14.

Use bolts between ¼ inch and ⅜ thick. Drill two holes through the notched area as in Fig. 18-15.

132

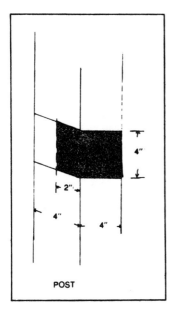

Fig. 18-12. A notch for a 4″ post.

On the side of the post that will face toward the *back* of your sign, drill a countersunk hole a little larger than the nut and as deep as the nut is thick. Hammer your carriage bolts in from the front and tighten the nuts with a socket wrench.

Hanging Sign

Usually the sign is centered under the horizontal arm between the vertical post and the end of the arm. Use appropriate-size screw eyes for the bottom of the post and open screw eyes for the sign. If

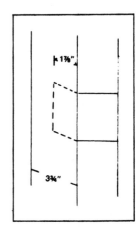

Fig. 18-13. An example of notch one-half the width of the post.

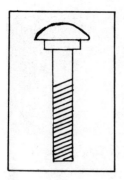

Fig. 18-14. Carriage bolt. The bolt is held in place by the square section beneath the head being sunk into the post by a hammer. The nut can then be tightened without holding the top with a wrench. The finished job is much neater with carriage bolts.

you want it to hang lower, put a couple of links of chain in between. It will hang well and swing gently in the breeze.

I know one gentleman who put lag bolts through the post and into the sign to prevent theft. A gale came along and tore the sign right off the bolts.

To help prevent theft, cement the post in the ground and have a couple of spikes in the post and under the cement. Also you can close the open eye with a small vise or weld it shut. Steel posts are also added insurance.

Figures 18-16 through 18-18 show examples of signs done with a router.

COLONIAL CANDLE STAND

In the early days of America when people used candles as a source of light, the candle stand was very popular because it could be moved to wherever the light was needed. As the trend to more

Fig. 18-15. Placement of carriage bolts.

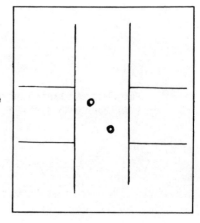

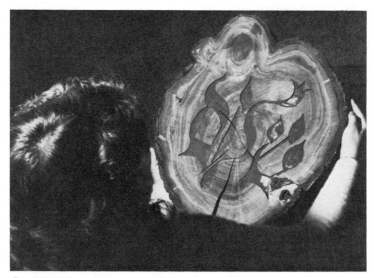

Fig. 18-16. Shalom on cross-cut walnut.

ornate furniture escalated, the functional candle stand kept pace. The traditional candle stand is one that has an octagon top, a spindle post, and the foot that is typically colonial—four heavy pieces set up like a plus sign. The standard dimensions are 25 inches high with a 13-inch top. See Fig. 18-19.

Fig. 18-17. A walnut slab.

Fig. 18-18. "Tir Tairngiri" Gaelic saying meaning something like "place of fulfillment." This sign is not finished. The initial has yet to be put at the bottom.

The candle stand shown in Fig. 18-20 is a free-form adaptation. I put it together so as to give you an idea of what might drive the curator of the Metropolitan Museum of Art up a wall. The candle stand shown in Fig. 18-20 is not sanded or finished because I made it

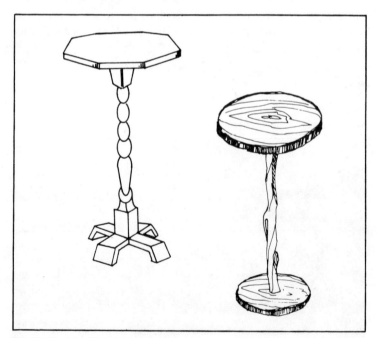

Fig. 18-19. A traditional candle stand is shown with its free-form counter part.

Fig. 18-20. A free-form candle stand.

to sit on the back deck this summer and for holding a pitcher of gin and tonic. I'll sand it someday when the pitcher runs dry.

There are innumerable variations of this stand. The base has an 8-inch, cross-section cut. The post can be a branch or anything that strikes your fancy. The top here is also a cross cut. In this case, I used cypress. The bottom is attached with glue and a long screw up from the underside into the post. The top was glued and doweled in place. If you put some thought, imagination, and effort in the candle holder, it will blend very beautifully with your Early American furniture.

137

Chapter 19

Trestle Table

The trestle table might be considered the backbone of the early American look. When combined with the free-form style, it becomes attractive and very authentic looking. For the one I made, even though I had walnut and oak available, I used pine and stained it dark. It could not have looked more early American if it had been passed down from 1776. See Table 19-1 for a material list.

Start with the tabletop. With luck, you will be able to find a single slab about 5' long and 33" to 34" wide, and an inch or more thick. It should preferably be about 2" or 3" thick with the free-form edges undisturbed. You are more apt to find a single slab of oak this big than any other wood. If you can find slabs of about 18" or 19" wide, and use two of them for the top.

The usual method of doing this is to "matchbook" them. See Figs. 19-1 and 19-2. This method lets you use two or more boards and keep the free-form edge on only the outside. As shown in Fig. 19-1, have the log slabbed so that one cut is in the dead center. The board on either side of this cut will be the two that you will want to use. Taking the slabs out of the center gives you two boards that are just about the same width and are relatively identical twins. The curvature of the free edge will match when you put them together, the slope of the bark on the edge will go in the same directions. If need be, you can use two boards that are not of center cut, but are from one side of the log. They will work, but the slopes of the free edge will not be of the same slope or angle and the curves on the free edge will not match exactly. If it is all you have, it will still make a nice table if you don't mind a little mismatch.

Table 19-1. Trestle Table Material List.

Table Top:	60″ × 33″ - 34″
Legs:	(2) 2″ × 8″ × 27″
Feet:	(2) 2″ × 6″ × 30″
Stretcher:	(1) 2″ × 4″ × 51″ - 53″
Cleats:	(2) 2″ × 4″ × 30″

When you have the two slabs, place them together just as they were in the tree. Select the edge you want to use and stand the boards up with the preferred edge up. Open the two pieces as you would a book. The matching edges will now be on the outside. Select the side of the boards you want as the tabletop. As the pieces lay now, you can use that side as you see it or the underside. You can't use the up side of one board and the down side of the other if you want the edges to be twins. Select the side to use due to the beauty of grain or the absence of imperfections in the face of the wood or even the slope of the sides or bark.

Next you are ready to square and cut off the uneven edges that will be in the middle of your tabletop. Use a chalk line or a large, *straight* piece of wood to draw a line lengthwise along and close to the edge. Make sure that you keep the width of the piece even. Cut

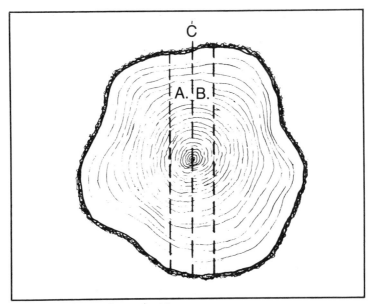

Fig. 19-1. Areas of a ''matchbook'' cut.

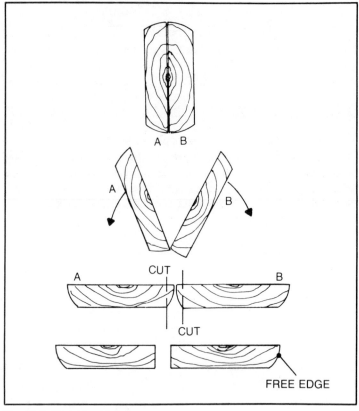

Fig. 19-2. "Matchbook" slabs.

along the line with a circular saw. You can use a handsaw if you are careful to make a straight cut. Do this with the matching edge of the other piece.

Try to make both pieces the same width or at least as close as possible. Place the pieces with the newly cut edges together leaving a ¼" separation between them. Temporarily hold them in this position by nailing a few 1"-×-2" strips on the back (Fig. 19-3). Be careful the nails do not come through the top.

This will help you keep the newly cut edges pressed closely together so that when you sand the top you do not unconsciously slip off and round those edges. Also with the two boards held together in the position that you want your tabletop, it is easy to square off the ends (if need be). I suggest that you make all cuts on this table square. Do not bevel the ends at all because the rest of the table will be basically 90-degree angles, except for the free-form edges.

LEGS

The legs should be at least 2″ stock and 8″ wide. Cut the legs to the exact length you want. The table should be 31″ high for the kitchen and could be 32″ for the dining room. Subtract the thickness of the top and the feet from the overall height and make the legs that length. For example, if your wood is 2″ thick and you want your table 31″ high, take off 2″ for the top, 2″ for the feet, and subtract 4″ from 31″ (you should get 27″). Make the legs exactly that length. Sand both sides.

If the free edges are relatively straight, you will probably want them positioned on the table so that the bevels of the free edge face in opposite directions. There is no rule about this because if you have only one place to put your table—for example, in a corner or with the narrow end against a wall—you would want the free edge positioned on both legs facing out so that the "free form" is more readily seen.

In order to get the end cuts straight, draw a chalk (or pencil) line down the center of your leg. If the sides are straight and even, you have no problem. If they are bent in any way (see Fig. 19-4), you will have to determine how you want the legs to sit. Off the center

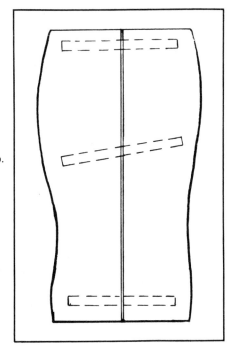

Fig. 19-3. Braces for the top.

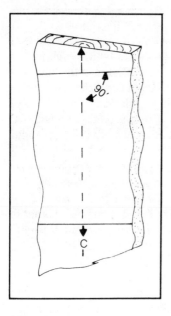

Fig. 19-4. Squaring the legs.

line, take a square line, top and bottom, using a T-square (not a book cover.) Measure again and double check the distance. Cut one end, cut on the waste side of the line you drew. Remeasure. If your other line is off, redraw it. Cut the other end on the waste side of that line. Again, measure.

If your leg is exactly the length you wanted, cut the other one the same length. If the first leg cut measures shorter than the 27″ you wanted, cut the second leg exactly the same amount shorter also. You can use the first leg as a template for the second. Your table will be a bit lower, but at least it will be level. You are not finished with these yet, but put them aside for awhile and you'll get back to them.

CLEAT

Next work on the boards that attach to the underneath of the table holding the top to the legs. These are called *cleats*. You can use cleats cut out of the same wood you are doing the whole table from or you can use pieces of 2″ × 4″. These will not be seen except by those crawling under the table to retrieve a dropped fork. If you cut these from your own wood, make them a full 2″ × 4″ and 4″ shorter than the width of your table. If you use a piece of 2″ × 4″, cut it also 4″ shorter than the width. It will measure 1¾″ × 3¾″ (width minus 4″). This is acceptable.

142

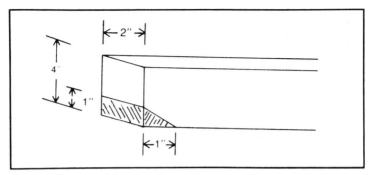

Fig. 19-5. Chamfer of braces.

I prefer to cut my own and make the 2″ side of the 2″ × 4″ the exact same width as the legs. Cut your cleats to the proper length. Fasten them to the table by the narrow side. You want to chamfer the corners off the "down" side. If your cleat is a full 2″ wide, measure down half the distance (or 1″ on each side of the corner). See Fig. 19-5. Join the lines across the wide side of the board and make the cut. This will give you a clean 45-degree corner.

The next step is for both strength and a neat job. You are going to join the leg to the cleat with a *rabbet* joint. See Fig. 19-6.

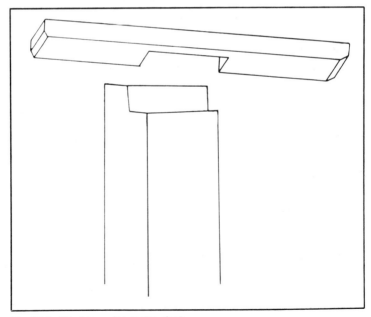

Fig. 19-6. Attaching a leg to the cleat.

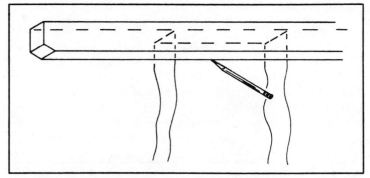

Fig. 19-7. Measuring for the cuts in the leg and the cleat.

LEG RABBET

This is not difficult to do if you are careful. Take the top of your leg, place the cleat against it—square and flush top to top. The part of the cleat that will be against the table top will be flush with the top of the leg. You want the cleat on the side of the leg that will be facing out. Mark it with a sharp pencil. See Fig. 19-7.

Take the very top of the leg and measure exactly one-half the distance of the width. Mark this along the top of the leg. You want to cut out this piece between the two lines. I will assume that your mark down the face of the leg is 4″. Cut down the grain 4″ deep. Then cut across the grain on the front of the leg to meet the other cut. The piece falls out and you have half of your rabbet.

Again place the cleat against the leg in the same position. Make sure the leg is perfectly centered with the cleat. Mark the inside of the cleat from the sides of the leg and across the 4″ width. Along the top of the cleat, draw a line between the two marks you just made at exactly ½ the width of the cleat (about 1″). Make several cuts the same depth between these outside cuts. You can then chisel out the waste. Do this to the other cleat (putting your notch on the inside also). Your legs and cleats are almost finished. Let's tackle the feet.

FEET

The feet should be about 6″ wide and they can be 2″ to 4″ thick. If you use the same stock you used for the legs and top, cut a piece 30″ × 6″ and cut a *chamfer* on the ends as you did on the cleats. Do not worry about having a "free-form" edge on the feet. If you prefer, you could have the free edge run along the outside of each foot. But then you might want to apply a principle of fashion; if you have big feet, don't call attention to them.

144

STRETCHER

The last piece is the stretcher that extends from leg to leg. Do it right for an authentic trestle table. Extend the stretcher through the legs and peg them on the outside. Does that seem difficult? It does take time and patience, but with very careful measuring it can be done. Make the stretcher 9″ shorter than the length of your table. Using the same 2″ stock, cut a piece 4″ wide and 9″ shorter than the table.

If you want to leave a free edge on this you can, but it is not necessary. If you do use the free edge, you have the option of facing it up or down. I suggest down. That way people will not chip it as readily if they put their feet on the top of it. As you see from where the free edge would go if you use one, the narrow or 2″ side faces up and down.

You are ready to cut out the end tenons. Measure in 5½″ from each end and draw a line on the 4″ face. Then from the top and bottom, measure 1″ down and mark this off from the end to your 5½″ mark. Cut out the two corner rectangles. You now have your tenons. Do the same to the other end. See Fig. 19-8.

No you can put a slight chamfer along both edges of the top side of the stretcher. I would say go in only about ¼″ and use a hand plane to shave it off. Be careful to not dig into the wood. Put the piece in a vise or nail 2 × 4s to a work bench and hold the piece tightly. Set the blade on the plane very shallow and use long, even strokes the whole length of the side. Your pencil marks, as described earlier, will keep you from going too deep. You are not finished with this piece, but put it aside for the moment.

MORTISES

Now go back to the legs. You still have to put holes in them (mortises) through which the tenons on the stretcher will fit. Mea-

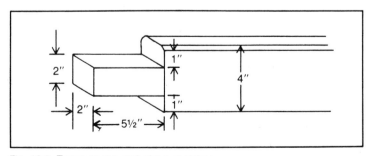

Fig. 19-8. Tenon on the end of the stretcher.

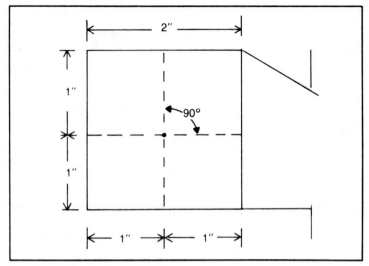

Fig. 19-9. Measuring for the tenon.

sure up from the bottom of the leg exactly 12″. Draw a line across the leg parallel to the bottom. Find the exact center of the leg on this line. Because the tenon on your stretcher is exactly 2″ square, this is what you want your mortise to be. So measure 1 inch above and below your 12″ line and also measure 1 inch on each side of your center line. Draw the square as in Fig. 19-9.

Do the same to the other leg. There are a couple of ways to cut the holes. If you have a power sabre saw with a blade long enough to reach all the way through your 2″ stock, you can very easily use it by drilling a hole within the square and cutting out the square. Cut along the *inside* of the lines to insure a tight fit of the tenon. You could also do this with a hand jig saw if you do not have an electric one. The third option, and by far the hardest, is to drill holes all the way around the inside of your square—each hole just about touching, but not quite—the line. Drill these holes as close as possible. Chisel out the middle piece and then clean up the sides with the chisel. Don't go all the way through from one side. Instead go half way through from one side and turn the leg over and do the other side. This avoids chipping the bottom side if you do the whole process from the top. You will have to draw your square on both sides if you do it this way.

A tip on getting the square on both sides to match is to draw it on one side and drill a small hole through the wood at the intersection of the center line and the line parallel to the bottom of the leg. You will have to use a jig or a drill press or something to insure a straight hole. There is no way anyone can drill a perfectly true perpendicular hole when holding a drill by hand and eyeballing it. With a true hole, you get your center point on the other side of the wood exact and you can draw the square off of it using the bottom of the leg to position it properly. I recommend the saw method.

With the hole in one leg, make sure the square drawn on the other leg matches perfectly. If it does, do your thing in cutting the hole. Sand the cut but do not round the edges. Now take the stretcher and place the tenon into the mortise of the proper leg. If the fit is too tight, use a file and work the opening of the mortise a bit more. It would be easier to sand the tenon down instead, but you will then get unmatching sides.

PEG AND PEG HOLE

When both sides fit snugly, the tenon is positioned all the way to shoulder. It is in the hole to the position where the wider part of the stretcher is touching the leg. Mark the top and bottom of each tenon using the outside of the leg as a guide. This will serve as a starting point for pegs that go through the ends of the stretcher. You must now put a vertical hole in each tenon so that you can peg it. In order to make the pegs fit tightly, it would be a good idea, at this point, to make the pegs before cutting the holes. Because your stretcher is 2″ thick, you want the pegs about ½″ thick. Because you have only 2½″ of stretcher extending out of the leg, you want your widest part of the peg no more than 1½″ wide. Because you are pegging 2″ thick stretcher and the middle 2″ of your peg will be hidden in the tenon, you want about 1½″ of peg extending out top and bottom. Make your peg 5″ long.

Your peg is ½″ × 1½″ × 5″. Cut two pegs to these dimensions. Measure down 1½″ from the top and make a shallow saw cut in the ½″ face. On the same side as the above saw cut, measure in ½″ along the bottom. Mark the spot and draw a line from this spot to the saw cut. Saw along this line and remove the outside piece. See Fig. 19-10.

Round the top from the cut to the top of the peg. Do not round the back. This will fit against the leg. You can combine all the measuring and cutting into two steps if you so prefer. Now make the other peg in the same way. Check to make sure both pegs are the same when you finish.

147

Check accurately the width and thickness of the pegs. This will determine the dimensions of the holes you have to cut in the tenons to fit the pegs into. Assuming the peg is ½" thick and tapered to the above dimensions, you are ready to draw the hole to be cut out. From the line you drew off the leg when the tenon was in place, you will want a ½" hole that will be 2" long and extending toward the outside end of the tenon. See Fig. 19-11.

If you want to insure a snug fit, move the hole 1/16" toward the center of the stretcher. When you put the peg in it will pull tight. Now cut the hole. You could drill a ½" hole at both ends and cut it with a sabre saw or you could drill ½" holes all the way down the 2" slot and clean out the waste with a chisel. Do this to both tenons. Having sanded everything completely, you are now ready for the assembly steps.

ASSEMBLY

Feet. To assemble your table work from the bottom up. Almost all of the joints will be glued as well as held with screws or dowels. I will discuss using screws, but you are free to use dowels instead if you want a table that you can brag has no hardware. Find the center of the feet and position the legs equidistant from sides and ends. Draw a light pencil line on the foot around all sides of the

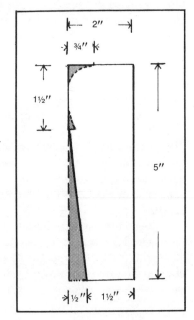

Fig. 19-10. A peg.

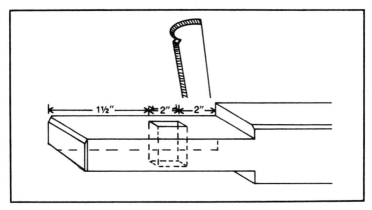

Fig. 19-11. A peg in a mortise.

leg. Do this on both feet and compare so that they match. Within the area to be covered by the legs, use a small piece of rough sandpaper to rough up the surface a bit. This provides a better bed for the glue to adhere.

Now drill 4 pilot holes for your screws. Use a bit slightly smaller than the shaft of the screw. Measure 1″ each side of your center point. Drill two holes; keep them on the center line. Measure out 1½″ from these holes and drill two more holes. Turn over the foot and gouge out with a penknife or a hand drill the top of the holes so that you can countersink the screws.

When both feet are finished, place the leg upside down in a vise and place the foot on it so that it lines up perfectly with the rectangle you penciled in. In case you have a free edge on the feet, make sure you have the grooves on the top of the legs corresponding properly to the free edge. The free edge of the foot should be on the same side of the leg as the groove for the rabbet at the top end of the leg.

Hold it in place with two nails placed through the two outside drilled holes and hammered about ¼″ into the leg. Drill the pilot holes into the leg through the other two holes. Keep your pilot hole about ⅜″ shorter than the screw you are using. I suggest you use about 4″ long screws for the feet and legs. Insert nails into the two holes you just made and repeat for the other two holes.

Remove the nails and coat the base of the leg and part of the foot that will be covered by the leg with glue. Use a good wood glue and follow the manufacturer's directions. Replace the foot and put the screws in. Make sure that all are tight. The stability of your table depends on them. Wipe off the excess glue and put the leg right side up and dry. Don't move it at all until it is *completely* dry.

149

Cleats. The only point to keep in mind when you attach these is to make sure you have the chamfer facing down. Place the cleat in position on the leg and drill three countersunk screw holes going from the leg side into the cleat, but not completely through. Use screws that are about ⅛" shorter than the thickness of the cleat and leg together. Glue both sides of the rabbet and screw together. Do both cleats.

Stretcher. Now put the stretcher in place. Make sure the chamfer is up. You know it fits well because you tried it when you cut the mortise. Glue the mortise of both legs and glue the part of the tenon that will remain inside the mortise. With the legs upright on their feet, work the tenons into place. Make very sure they are all the way in.

Pegs. Put some glue on the middle part of your pegs and in their holes. Gently hammer them in to the point where the part extending out the top is about equal amount as that extending out the bottom. Wipe away all excess glue.

Top. Lay the tabletop face down on a clean work bench or floor and place the leg assembly on it at its approximate position. Adjust the position so that the outside of the cleats are equidistant from the ends of the table and all four ends of the cleats are also the same distance from the sides of the table. This will ensure you that the top is square on the leg assembly.

If you have clamps to fit, clamp the cleat in place. Be sure to put a smooth buffer board under the table and over the cleat so that the ends of the clamp won't dig into your table. If you don't have clamps, pencil mark around the cleats so that, if you inadvertently move the leg assembly, you will see it. Drill through the cleat into the table about a distance of one-half the thickness of the stock. To make sure that you do not drill too far, measure the thickness of the cleat and the distance you want to go into the tabletop and measure that combined distance up the drill bit. Put a piece of masking tape around the bit; expose below it the distance you want.

When you drill, stop when the masking tape reaches the cleat. Your hole is the perfect depth. Drill two holes on each side of the leg and use only screws of the proper length. Do *not* use glue for this connection. This allows the larger boards some movement without breaking anything if they are exposed to extreme temperatures or humidity. It also allows for future mobility insofar as the top can be removed for transporting or even refinishing. Now you can remove the thin strips you put on if your top was more than one board.

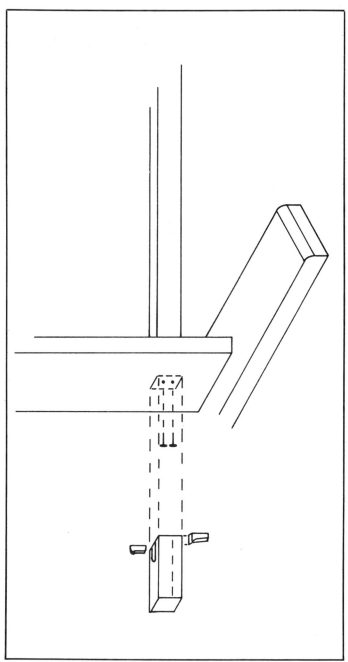

Fig. 19-12. A fake peg in a tenon.

Finish. The last step is to go over the whole table with fine sandpaper. This is especially important for the parts that had glue on them. If even a trace of glue remains, the spot will not take a stain. Apply the preferred finish.

Addenda. Here are a few ways to cheat. For the pegs, you can use a piece of ⅝" dowel. This will save you from digging out the hole. Instead you can merely drill a ⅝" hole and hammer the dowel through. Or you could make the legs solid with no mortise for the stretcher and make the stretcher itself without the tenons and just long enough to fit perfectly between the legs. For this particular table, you would make it 11" shorter than the dimensions given. Attach the stretcher with glue and by countersunk screws (two on each side) from the outside of the leg into the ends of the stretcher. On the outside of the leg, matching up with the stretcher is glued a piece of 2" × 2⅝" with the top and bottom piece of peg glued on to look authentic. This eliminates the cutting of all holes. See Fig. 19-12.

Chapter 20

Picnic Table

There is a growing need for garden and backyard furniture. Building your own picnic table is less expensive than buying one. You can make one nicer and more period oriented than you can buy. I have never seen a free-form picnic table on the market. Actually, I have never seen one at all except the one I built. See Figs. 20-1 and 20-2.

If you build a table of redwod or cedar, it will last a lifetime. But the wood might be either unavailable or the price might be prohibative. Any other wood you use should be treated with wood preservative or painted. See Table 20-1 for a material list.

BUILDING THE PIECES

First cut out the four legs. Cut the correct angle with a compass. Next cut the bench arms 52″ long and cut a little bevel on the ends as shown in Fig. 20-3. The angle is not important as long as it's not too radical. Make the three cleats; put about a 60° bevel on the ends. Don't make the braces until the table is completely together.

You have an option for the top. If you happen to have a slab about 30″ wide, you are lucky and it will make a great top. If not use two or more slabs. You have the option of squaring off all the center sides or leaving the free edge on all the boards and placing them as close as possible. I squared mine off because the free edge was so irregular that I felt the spaces were too large between them. I left the free edge on each outside edge, and I left ½″ between each board.

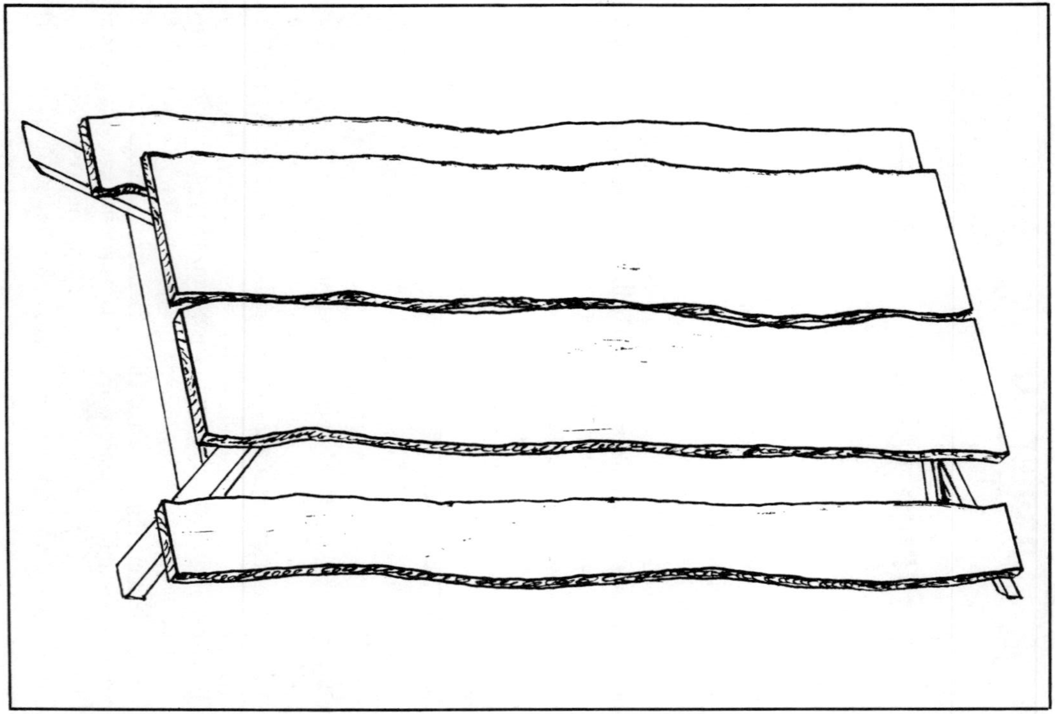

Fig. 20-1. A picnic table.

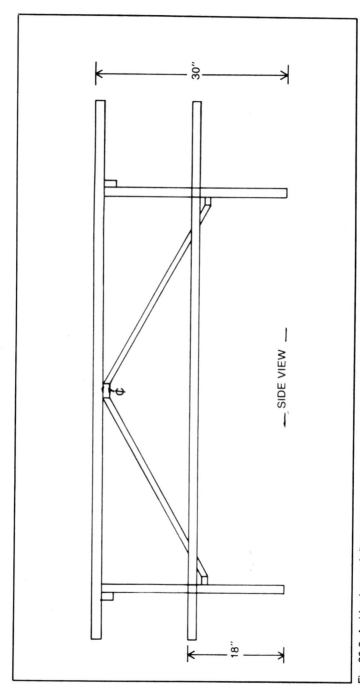

Fig. 20-2. A side view and dimensions.

Table 20-1. Material List.

Top:	2 pieces 2× 14 (15) × 74
Seat:	2 pieces 2 × 10 (12) × 74
Two End Cleats:	3 pieces 4 × 4 × 29
One Center Cleat:	1 piece 2 × 4 × 29
Bench Arms:	2 pieces 4 × 4 × 52
Braces:	2 pieces length as required
Legs:	4 pieces 4 × 4 × 33

2 ×s can be substituted for 4 × 4s for a lighter table

To make the bench, use a slab 10″ × 12″ wide. You can leave the free form intact or square off the inside if you prefer. If you need two slabs for the bench, square the centers (or not) so as to match the top. If leaving the free edge intact will make the bench wider than 12″ or create a space between the two pieces that is uncomfortable to sit on, you will be forced to square them off. Sand all pieces fully before construction.

CONSTRUCTION

Lay the top out—upside down—and install each end cleat 6″ from the ends of the table. The tabletop will hang over a full 6″. Put six flat-head wood screws in each cleat. If you use more than 2 slabs for the top, make sure that there are at least two, if not three, screws in each slab. If you use 2 × 4 cleats, use 2 ½″ screws. If you use anything heavier, use screws long enough to extend at least half way

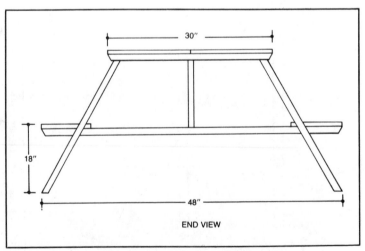

Fig. 20-3. The end view and dimensions.

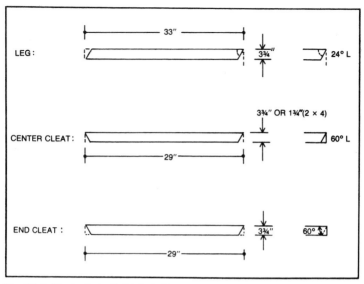

Fig. 20-4. Dimensions of cleats in legs.

into your top boards. Of course, all these screws go into the cleat and through to the slabs. If you want to put them through the top and into the cleat, you should countersink them and use "fade" dowels to finish it off. I usually avoid this with furniture that will be out in the weather.

Assemble the leg sections (the two legs and the seat bench arms). Attach the arms on the inside of the legs and then secure with ¼-×- 4 or 8″ carriage bolts. Use a flat washer under the nut.

Secure each leg section to the *inside* of the cleat on each end and again use carriage bolts.

Secure the seat for each bench and use flat-head wood screws.

Cut the braces to fit between the bench arm and the center cleat. Make it fit snugly and secure it with lag bolts or wood screws. See Fig. 20-4.

Be sure to be liberal in coating all surfaces of your table with wood preservative. Paint, stain, and finish to your own preference. If you use varnish, make sure it is for *exterior* use.

Barbecue some chicken and have plenty of your favorite beverage. Enjoy!

Chapter 21

Surface Treatments

The surface condition of a piece of wood probably depends on how it was cut. For example, a chain saw cut usually is rougher than the cut from a sawmill blade. If the board is too rough or uneven, you can save some time and money if you take it to a mill and have it planed. Possibly it would cost you less for this planing than for the sandpaper that would be necessary to bring the wood to the smoothness of the planed board.

SANDING

In most cases, I like to do the sanding before I attach the legs. This allows me to push and lean on the board while sanding it without worrying about weakening the leg joints. It also gives me the freedom to change my mind and use the other side of the board should I find some flaw in the grain after sanding.

You can build an unusual piece, but if your sanding is sloppy or incomplete, your finish will look amateurish—if not downright sloppy. The most important step in finishing furniture is the preparation for sanding the wood. Whether your finish is transparent or paint, it will reflect the surface, magnify any imperfections, and show the world just how much effort and care you put into it. Your expertise as a furniture maker will be judged more from the condition of the finish than from the creativity of the piece.

The availability of power tools will help and will determine to some degree how many hours of work will be needed. If you have had your slab planed and can work it with a belt sander, you are in good shape. If you cut your piece with a chain saw and must work from there with no power tools, you have a job and a half ahead of you. It certainly can be done, but you might want to consider giving up jogging because you'll probably get more exercise than you need just in the sanding. Most commonly, a belt sander is used and then a hand finish is worked up.

If the piece is rough, use a rough-grit sandpaper and sand in all directions—cross-grain, diagonal, and finally with the grain—until the piece is relatively smooth. The only roughness that remains is the scratchy surface left by the rough sandpaper. Go to a medium-grit paper and use good judgment here. If the scratches come out by going with the grain, sand that way. If they do not come out, sand cross grain again, and then with the grain.

Switch now to a fine paper. Sand with the grain on this one. This principle applies whether you are using a belt sander or doing it by hand. Assuming that you used a sander, you still should work a satin finish by hand sanding. All hand sanding on flat surfaces should be done with a block so that indentations are not sanded into the surface. Any block can be used. You can take a 6-inch piece of 2 × 4 and wrap a piece of sandpaper around it; this will work fine. For your finish, use a very fine paper and work and rework the surface. Finish by rubbing it with pumice or rotten stone. Follow manufacturers' directions.

Here is a little tip that can add to the richness of your finish. I recommend this for a soft wood with a distinctive grain such as pine. When you have finished all sanding, rub the finished surface with a damp (not wet) cloth. Allow the surface to completely dry. This will cause the softer grain to absorb more moisture than the harder wood and thus swell more. Not before the surface is dry but not more than a few hours after, sand with a very fine sandpaper and do *not* use a block. With the paper under your fingers, let them follow the softer grain. Be sure to cover the complete piece as uniformly as possible. Repeat this with pumice or rotten stone. As the piece completely dries, the softer sanded grain will slightly recess. This gives much more character to the wood.

FILLERS

Using a filler is basically a matter of choice. Some say that fillers hide the grain. Others say that they accentuate the grain. Still others say that you take away the naturalness of the wood. If you do not yet have a preference, experiment with a filler. Older cabinet-makers preferred to fill open-grained wood such as oak. Some used a filler to match the tone and others contrasted the tone to bring out the grain (white filler).

Some fillers come ready to use and some you have to mix. Once ready to use, it should be applied to a small area at a time and allowed to partially dry. At that point, it should be wiped with a clean, dry soft cloth. First wipe against the grain, then in a circular motion, and finally with the grain. Allow to dry at least the time recommended by the manufacturer. Sand with very fine paper, with the grain, until you achieve the preferred finish.

Apply a thin sealer to keep the filler from bleeding into your finish.

SEALERS

You can use a sealer on raw wood before a finish coat to provide more consistent coverage on the heartwood and sapwood. For example, on an unsealed crosscut section, it will take 10 or 12 coats of varnish on the sapwood before you get any coating at all. The heartwood, on the other hand, will begin to build up after three or four coats. A good sealer will help lessen this aggravating difference in absorption.

Some sealers can be applied before or after stain. Applied after stain, it does seal in the stain and, as all sealers, it will offer a better adhesive surface for the final finish. A sealer should always be used over filler. And all sealers should be worked lightly with very fine sandpaper before final coat.

Always use a sealer that is compatable with the finish you intend to use. If it is varnish, use a varnish sealer; use a lacquer sealer for a lacquer finish. Always try a combination, if you have not used it before, on scrap wood. It is possible that a lacquer could lift the filler that you sealed and sanded (sanded just enough possibly to break the seal). It's easier and smarter to try your combination on a piece of scrap than ruin your project. To correct such a mistake is time-consuming, nervewracking, and so unnecessary because it can be avoided.

You can make your own sealer from 1 part shellac and 2 parts alcohol. This will work over oil or alcohol base stains and accept a varnish finish over it.

STAIN

Assuming now that the entire piece is sanded to your satisfaction, you have a choice of finishes. Your first consideration must be whether to stain your material—all of it or part of it—or to put a natural finish on it.

Your decision will be dictated by the wood, the decor of the room where you intend to use the piece, or a tone you want to imitate or match. For example, you might want to stain pine to an Early American look and you might want to use a Jacobean shade. You might want to darken oak wood by using a dark oak or a middle tone stain. You can get a pine or maple wood close to a walnut color if you like.

Whatever you do with stain, you should choose your color carefully. To "fine tune" a tone, you will have to mix another color with it. You might want to mix a light and dark oak to get what you want. It is best to test this on a piece of scrap left over from your project. Make sure to sand it the same way and to the same texture that you sanded the finished piece. If the finish of your practice piece is a different texture, the stain will turn out a different shade.

When you are finding the tone, remember to try the various types of stain such as varnish stain, oil, alcohol, or water-base stain. Each will affect the tone slightly. You can lighten the tone by thinning the stain according to manufacturer's directions.

Decide how you want to apply the stain. You can use a brush, cloth, a terry towel, or possibly spread it with your hand. Each has its own merit. The brush is the neatest. A cloth or terry towel does rub some off as you put it on and this is all right if you want that tone. If you want a very dark tone, you apply a second coat or spread it with your hand. Cosmetically, using your hand is a bad idea but it does give good results. If you use your hand, it is advisable to wear a surgical glove. One walnut-colored hand is not always socially acceptable.

After you stain the piece, you can dry rub it with a cloth or terry towel. This will remove a bit of the stain from the harder wood grain, but not the soft wood grain, and it will bring out more of the beauty of the grain. The purpose of stain is to match wood or to change it to your taste. To cover up the grain is a shame unless you do that for some very specific reason. Try to accomplish your change of tone and keep as much grain as possible. Basically, I feel the purpose of stain is to highlight the grain in woods. I cannot emphasize enough that the secret of a good stain finish is a good sanding job. Stain will accentuate any scratch or flaw in the material; make it as perfect as you can.

There is a technique that you can use effectively with some woods. It is possible to stain a wood and then block sand lightly the harder grain, leaving the stain only in the soft wood. A cross cut or a diagonal cut of ash is a good example of a wood that accepts this technique well. Lampblack, Jacobean, and walnut stain are commonly used with this technique. Yet any shade can be used or your own shade can be mixed. I have mixed artists' oil paint with a light oak, oil-base stain and created a new color to match the piece. This works well as a full stain or a grain stain.

After you have tested the color, tone, types of stain, and method of application, you are ready to begin. Make sure that there is no wax, glue, or oil on your piece. The stain will accentuate these because the wood under them will not accept the dye.

For staining flat surfaces in a horizontal plane, it is best to start in the center and work toward the ends. In a vertical plane, such as the side of a cabinet or bookcase, work from the top down. Do not let any part dry before you blend into it.

One final note of caution is to try to have enough stain from the *same* can to finish the whole piece or set. Different manufacturers produce a stain with the same name that can vary greatly in tone. Even different batches from the same manufacturer can vary slightly.

FINISH

Some woods contain their own beauty that, in many cases, you want to preserve. In such cases, you have a choice of finishes to enhance the natural beauty. This can be achieved by the use of varnish, shellac, polyurethane, lacquer, rubbing oil, or some commercial plastic finish. All of these can be purchased in a ready-mixed form. It is extremely important to follow the manufacturers' instructions on how to use them.

Most of these finishes require more than one application and a light sanding in between coats. Whether you rough the finish with fine sandpaper, 400 and up, or steel wool, 00 and finer, use long sweeping motions with the grain of the wood so you won't build up heat. If this sanding is omitted, the bond between the two coats might not be strong and peeling might result. When the finish is completed, I prefer applying a furniture paste wax and buffing it with a wool cloth.

Select the finish you want. Each has its own merit. Varnish gives a greater luster to the finish, shellac changes the tone of the wood very little, lacquer lends itself to spray application and dries quickly, and oil is probably more work than the others. Each has its assets and drawbacks. Choose for the end result and not the work involved.

Most finishes are applicable over a stain finish and will enhance the tone and the grain even more. A rubbed oil or wax finish over a raw stain can lighten it a bit. Once this happens, it is too late to darken it with more stain because it will not take through the oil or wax. You are then stuck with what you have. Try it on scrap before you commit yourself.

One rather successful, but sloppy method of application of a varnish or polyurethane—that is not be mentioned in the manufacturers' recommendations—is to pour it on directly from the can. This will work only on a flat surface like a tabletop. Pour a liberal amount on the surface that you have set up as level as possible. Make sure all areas are covered equally. It should be thick enough to cover the whole area and run off, but no thicker.

If there are any bubbles, break or remove them with your finger. Remove any other imperfections such as specks of hard varnish that you picked up from the side of the can while pouring. Once it is poured, don't brush or wipe it. Just let it sit there and do its thing.

Allow it to run off the sides and smooth it on them or wipe it off as preferred. If the sides of your piece still have bark on them, you can dab the initial runoff into the bark and, if you didn't over do things with the pour, the remaining runoff will lose itself in the cracks of the bark. Be prepared to stay around for awhile and dab the sides. If the sides are smooth, you will want to let it run off and dry, and then sand it smooth when it is completely dry. Keep in mind that if the manufacturer recommends 24 hours to dry, the whole thing might take a few days longer because it is so thick. After a day, wipe the runs on the sides and break the columns and let it dry again. This will hasten the drying time.

Do all your finishing in as dust free a place as possible. Once you apply the finish, leave the area. A lot of movement will stir up dust you don't even see. Don't apply a finish in the same area where you were just sanding. The dust hangs for hours. I watched a friend of mine be very careful about finding a dust-free room to do his finishing. He took his new table to the room and proceeded to wipe and blow the dust from his piece before applying the varnish. I prefer to keep the doors and windows of an area closed for a few hours *before* I use it, as well as keep every one out. When I use the room, I move around as little as possible and try to wear clothing that gives off as little lint as possible.

When you are working with finishes, you should ventilate the room for health and safety purposes. The fumes are volatile. And they should not be inhaled in a closed room. It is advisable to apply the finish at as close to room temperature as possible (70° F) and never in direct sunlight. Direct sun or too hot a room will make your finish set up too quickly and it will not be smooth. It might even blister. Too cold a room can cause the finish to crack or become cloudy.

All this might seem a bit fanatical, but remember a poor finish can wreck a great piece of work. Considering all the time and labor you put into it, these few extra precautions will be well worth the effort.

If you want as perfect a finish as possible, here are a few steps to follow. First, buy a new brush 2 to 3 inches wide; it need not be the most expensive. A previously used brush is never clean no matter how good it looks.

Second, buy a new can of varnish. Old varnish does not set up well. Your varnish might not be that old and it still could be alright, but then it might not be good. You might have forgotten when you bought it or it might have been in a range of temperature that was not good for its stability. If you rebel against throwing it away, then use it on your woodshed. Do not use it on your new "labor of love" piece of furniture.

Third, buy a tack rag (or make your own). More about this in a bit.

Fourth, clean the surface by dusting well and move it to a relatively dust-free area. Go over *all* surface with the tack rag. For this fourth step, I am assuming the surface has been sanded, stained if necessary, sealed with shellac or lacquer and gone over lightly with a fine steel wool.

Fifth, pour the can of varnish into a big bowl and add about a quarter of a can of turpentine. Stir it up gently but completely. Brush it on firmly covering the entire surface with a liberal, but not too thick coat. When you have finished, scrutenize the surface by positioning yourself so that you newly varnished surface is between you and some source of light. If you see a dull spot, you missed it with the varnish. Add some to that area. Finish by using long brush storokes going with the grain. If there are bubbles, don't worry about them; they'll go away.

Last, pour the remaining varnish back into the can and put the lid on *tightly*. Store your brush in a clean can with turpentine completely covering all the bristles.

Allow the finish to dry the amount of time recommended on the can. When the finish is completely dry, go over it with steel wool, with the grain, rubbing hard enough to dull the surface but not so hard as to take off the coat you just put on. Clean the surface well and again use a tack rag on it. Apply another coat of the stuff you saved from the day before. Actually, one good coat will seal the surface well so you could stop there. You can put on as many coats as you want, but be very sure the previous coat is completely dry and be sure you use the steel wool treatment between each coat.

Finishing Touch

When your final coat is dry, rub it *with* the grain with either steel wool or pumice and a soft rag. Rub only hard enough to remove any minor imperfections that are on the surface, such as a piece of dust. Then wax with a good paste wax and buff it well with a soft cloth.

A note about the type of varnish you use is that one thing you must do in order to have a lasting good finish is to use the proper varnish for the right job. Use exterior or marine varnish *only* for outside projects. Don't be fooled into thinking that if it holds up outside it will be better and stronger inside. It is true that interior varnish can crack and peal if used outside. The reason is that it will not expand and contract with the changes of temperature.

On the other hand, exterior varnish, made to adjust to temperature changes, never really dries all the way through (or you might say it dries to a rubbery consistency). If you have a table finished with exterior varnish and put a plant on it for any length of time, it will make a dent in the varnish. Not so with interior. It dries hard. So even if you were in the navy, don't use marine varnish on your bar top. Use interior varnish for inside work and use exterior marine for outside. No exceptions.

You can put varnish over shellac or lacquer. Never put shellac over lacquer or varnish. If you use a varnish stain, you need not seal it further with shellac. Apply varnish directly because the sealer is in the stain itself.

Making a Tack Rag

Take a piece of clean rag (preferably cheesecloth). A relatively lint-free type will do. A piece about 2 feet by 2 feet is ideal. Put some varnish in a bowl and cut it with a bit (not much) of turpentine. Soak the rag in it and ring it out as much as you can. Put it in another clean dry rag and beat on it. You now have your tack rag. You can keep it indefinitely by storing it in a jar with an airtight lid.

PAINT

It is with very guarded language that I mention paint in a book about free-edge wood. To cover the grain and obliterate the natural beauty of a free-edge piece would be a desecration of the wood—and maybe even of nature, motherhood, and apple pie. But it certainly is valid to use a natural or stained piece of free-form wood in conjunction with a milled or painted piece. Examples are replacing the top of a regular office desk with free-edge wood or putting an oak counter top on painted cabinets in a kitchen. Free edge can be mixed with anything: painted wood or metal, formica, straight-edge wood, chrome, plastic, wrought iron, etc. The important thing is to be sure that the free-edge wood is the focal point of the piece. Your choice of paint should be considered carefully for color and gloss.

A high-gloss can detract from, rather than enhance, the natural wood. You might want a flat paint combined with a high-gloss finish on your wood or an oiled wood and a satin paint. The color should be neutral enough, in relation to the wood, so that it does not detract from it. It should at least contrast enough so that the wood does not look like an afterthought.

I put a free-edge ash slab on a metal desk, stained the ash with lampblack, and sanded it off—leaving the dark in the grain. The finish for the piece was a satin black paint for the desk and a high-gloss bar top varnish on the wood. This is a very attractive combination. Another combination that is rather attractive is a black walnut top on an off-white counter. A good way to give a facelift to a kitchen is to replace the doors on the painted kitchen cabinets with natural free-edge doors.

Combining some free edge to existing pieces can very well be an easy and inexpensive way to give a new look to the area. Be conscious of the relationships. I once saw a mahogany bar top on a red velvet, chrome, and mirror base. There was just too much to look at. The piece was "too busy."

A general rule is that you can mix wood with just about anything. If you want the wood to catch the eye, it will take cautious planning. I saw free-form legs used for a standing aquarium and they were used only to carry on the theme of the room. They were a good blend and in themselves did not stand out. They gave the fish tank the flavor of the room.

I am not saying that the non-wood portion must be plain and simple. I saw, in a restaurant, a solid, free-edge bar top about 15 feet long and 6 inches thick covering a large tank containing live trout. The tank was lighted and very attractive with its seaweed and rocks, and it was not plain and simple. At the same time, it did not clash nor detract from the wood top.

I have used free edge very successfully with used brick room dividers and fireplace walls, wrought iron legs, and glass tops. Don't by restricted by tradition. If you have an idea, try it.

SUMMARY OF FINISHES

Bleach. This is composed of various acids and chlorine compounds. It is usually very strong and should never come in contact with skin. It should be applied with a brush. It lightens wood, but it also removes the luster and makes the grain less intense. It is used to make wood, such as driftwood, blond and to give siding or paneling a weathered look.

Lacquer. This consists of resins, gums, cellulose derivatives, and solvents. The combination makes a very pleasing finish, but it is a very volatile compound. Never use it near an open flame such as a gas, hot-water heater or a cigarette. It is usually applied with a spraygun and it dries rapidly. It is hard, durable, and acid resistant. It comes in a glossy, satin, or dull finish and it is not recommended for outside wood finish.

Oil. Boiled linseed oil or various other commercial products are used. It is wiped or brushed on and allowed to sit, but it is wiped off before it gets tacky or sets up. The surface is immediately buffed well. This then is allowed to dry for several hours and rubbed with a very fine steel wool (0000) before the next application. The more applications the better. A good oil finish has 20 to 30 coats and then an application of a good paste furniture wax. This finish emphatically brings out the tone and grain.

The finish is a durable protection with a soft luster, but it must be renewed once or twice a year. Wash the piece with a wax-cutting solution, sand lightly, and oil in same manner as much as necessary to bring the finish back to its original look. Rewax. This finish does not guarantee against stain from glasses and spills.

Paint. Paint is composed of pigments suspended in linseed oil (oil-base paint), or in various synthetics (latex), or in varnish (enamel). It is applied with a roller, a brush, or a spray gun. It is hard, durable, and it obliterates tone and grain of wood.

Varnish. This is a clear, durable finish that comes in a high-gloss finish or satin finish, as well as interior, exterior, and bar top quality. The bar top is impervious to water and alcohol. It is applied with a brush or, less frequently, a spray gun. Follow manufacturers' directions carefully and sand lightly between coats. The more applications the better. Usually four or five coats are sufficient. Up to 20 coats make a remarkable glass-like finish after being rubbed with rotten stone and waxed.

Chapter 22

Vanity

The size of the cabinet will be determined by the space available and the size of the sink. The cabinet shown in this chapter was constructed out of leftover wood. This accounts for the varying thickness used. Because the sides were solid slabs, that is, not pieces fitted together, and the top was only two boards, I decided that the cabinet would be sturdy enough without building a 2 × 4 frame.

DIMENSIONS

The top of the cabinet should be a standard 30 inches off the floor. It can be as wide as you like. The bowl of the sink should be no more than 2 inches from the front edge of the cabinet. At the bottom front, there should be a 3″-×-3″ indentation for foot room. The depth of the cabinet will be determined probably more by space available than by taste. If you have the room, it is nice to have 6 or 9 inches in back of the bowl for toothpaste, etc. The cabinet pictured here does not have that feature. Of course, the depth must accommodate the sink and it should have an inch of wood in front of it. See Fig. 22-1.

CONSTRUCTION

Having determined the dimensions, lay out the pieces to be cut.

Top

The sink used here was round and 19 inches in diameter. I wanted the bowl to be against the back of the cabinet with a 1-inch space in front and the top ½ inch countersunk into the splash panel. So the depth had to be 20½ inches. The width is 28¾". The stock was shy of an inch (about 15/16). Cut the top to size and have the free edge on the front. Measure in from the back edge ½ inch. Draw a line across the back. This will be the area sunk into the splash board. From this line, measure out 9½ inches (one half the width of your sink). Mark this line. Find the center from the sides. Mark this.

At this point, drive a nail at the intersection. This will be the center of your bowl. Determine how much lip is around the edge of the bowl so that you can decide how much edge to leave on the wood for the sink to sit on. On the particular sink I had, I left a ½ inch lip. The circle that I cut out was 18 inches in diameter. Draw this around the center point that you have marked.

If you don't have a compass large enough to draw the circle, use a piece of string, loose loops on each end, forming a 9-inch radius. With a pencil on the outside, go around the circle. Careful not to stretch the string more on one side than the other. Instead of a perfect circle, you might get a deformed egg. Cut out the circle with a sabre saw and the hole you have should allow your bowl to sit snugly with a sufficient lip to support the sink. See Fig. 22-2.

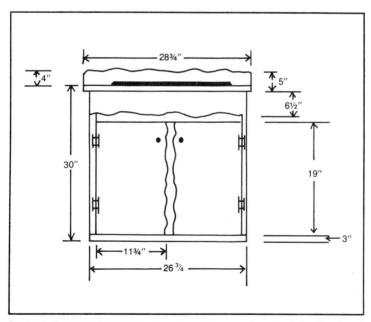

Fig. 22-1. The height and width of a cabinet. They can be adjusted to the size of the bowl and the space available.

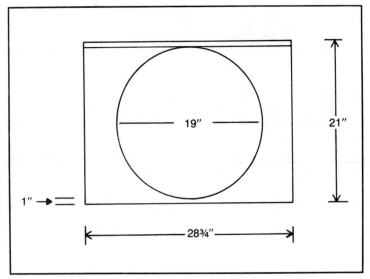

Fig. 22-2. The dimensions of the top of the cabinet. The dimensions can be adjusted accommodating varying bowl sizes and space available.

Sides

Cut the sides to dimension. You should have pieces wide enough to get the complete side without piecing boards together. The ones I used were 19" by 29" high. Because the right side of my cabinet would be hidden in a corner, I used ⅝" plywood for that to save my free-form wood. Cut out the 3"-×-3" notch at the bottom.

On the plywood side, I cut off ½" from the front in order to glue on a strip of wormy pine and match the other side. The pine side was 1¼ inch stocks so I glued and nailed a piece ½" × 1¼" to the front of the plywood. Looking straight at the cabinet, the sides now matched. Don't bother to run the strip below the 3 × 3 cut out at the bottom. The kickboard will take care of this. See Fig. 22-3.

SPLASH BOARD

Have the splash board extend about 4" above the top. The best joint here is to notch the splash board to accept the top and glue and screw it. Make the board exactly as wide as the top (in this case 28¾ inches wide). Because the top here was about 1" stock and you want about 4" showing, make the board 5" wide. For this I used 1" stock. Cut your notch ½" deep and the width of the top. Make sure the top and splash board are well sanded before you put them together. See Fig. 22-4.

ATTACHING SIDES

With the sides sanded, attach the top to them. You can do this rather easily with angle brackets on the under side of the top and inside the side pieces. Also glue the top to the sides.

FACEPLATE

For the want of a better term, I will call the board that goes across the front of the cabinet directly under the top the faceplate. This is, in this cabinet, 26¾″ × 6½″. It should sit on the end pieces and be flushed with the outside of the sides. It can have a free edge on the bottom part. Glue and fasten the plate into place. You can use dowels or countersink screws with the holes plugged. If you are in a hurry, countersink finishing nails. All the pieces are fine sanded

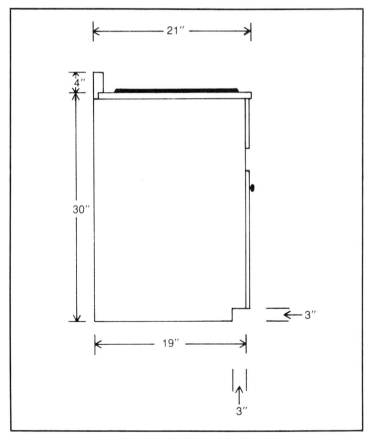

Fig. 22-3. Dimensions of the side (height and depth).

before installation. I used ⅝″ stock for this and the doors. Both should be the same thickness.

KICKBOARD

This is the piece at the bottom that your toe will kick when you stand at the cabinet. It will kick it if you stand too close or if you have big feet. The piece fits against the inside of the end pieces so it is shorter than the faceplate that extends to the outside of them. In this case, it was 24¼″ × 3″. Attach this to the bottom with glue and dowels or countersink screws or nails.

SHELF

A shelf on the bottom will help hold the whole thing together without braces. If you do not want a shelf, then brace the back at the bottom. If you do use a shelf, check the drain and water pipes. If they come out of the floor, you will have to make cutout slots for them in the shelf. If the pipes come from the wall, things are a bit more easy. If both sides of this cabinet are 1¼″ stock, the shelf will be an easy 24½″ and 19″ deep. In my case, I had to add 1⅛″ to compensate for my one ⅝″ plywood side. I used ⅝″ plywood for the shelf. Cut it out and install it. You can use angle brackets under the shelf to hold it in place.

BORDER FOR DOORS

You must install a border along the top of the doors and a center post for them to butt against. I used scrap pieces of the same wood for these. Sand before installing. Both were of ½″ stock. The top piece was 3″ wide and extended from side to side. Cut it to the exact inside measurement. About 1 inch of the 3 inches was behind and butting against the facing board. The rest extended below to fill the space between that faceboard and the top of the doors. Put a few small screws through this board into the back of the facing board and then toenail (from the back into the sides).

In the exact center of your cabinet, you need a center post. This fills the space between the doors and, as does the top, acts as a stop for them. Have this post run from the bottom of the top board that you just installed to the bottom of the shelf. Match the shelf so that the post extends to the bottom. Glue and nail it here and use a T-brace at the top. Allowing 2½″ should be plenty wide for this piece.

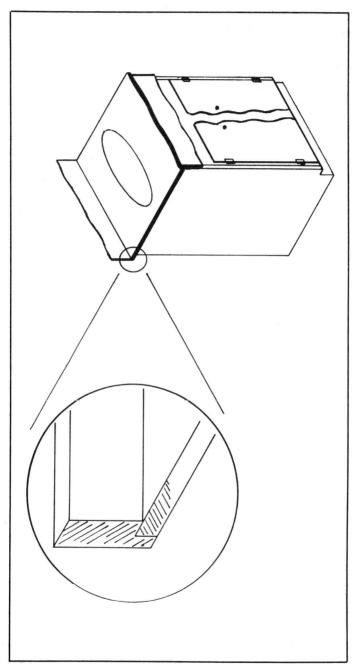

Fig. 22-4. A cabinet and a cutaway of the joint for connecting the splashboard to the top.

Fig. 22-5. A cabinet with free-edge pine. Many worm holes were used. This finish is natural with a high-gloss varnish applied.

DOORS

I left the free edge on the center part of the doors. Your doors extend from the bottom line of the shelf to within an inch or one-half inch of the facing board. The dimensions of these doors are 19″ × 11¾″. I used ⅝″ stock; it is the same as the facing board. After completely sanding the front and sides of each door, I attached them with offset hinges to the edges of each side with the screws provided. On the inside and at the top, I put magnets to hold the doors shut. Stain and finish to your preference. Clamps and directions are provided for installing the sink. The plumbing is up to you. Good luck! See Fig. 22-5.

Chapter 23

Fireplace Mantel

Do you like a heavy, large mantel or something less than massive? See Fig. 23-1. Do you prefer the mantel extending the complete width of the brick or stone facing or do you like it just over the firebox? If you are not sure, I suggest you look at pictures of other fireplaces.

The next consideration should be the decor. What is the rest of the room like? Modern or semimodern settings might not lend themselves to a massive free-form mantel or, for that matter, any other kind of free-form design.

Installation in the new construction is by far the easiest. By new construction, I do not mean a brand new house or a completely new room. I mean only the fireplace even if it is an old house in which you are installing a new fireplace.

PLANNING AHEAD

If you are having the fireplace built by a contractor, know how wide the facing will be and how far out you want the mantel to extend, how long you want it, and how thick you would like it. You might find the kind you want at a sawmill or the mill might be able to cut to order the piece you want. I took my own pine log to the mill and had it cut. When you have your piece, sand it, stain it, varnish it, or leave it rough—whatever you want. But make sure it is completely finished before installation.

Have it handy for the contractor to see it and measure it before he starts the brick or stone face. The reason for this is that a

Fig. 23-1. A complete fireplace with a free-form mantel.

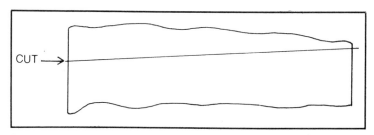

Fig. 23-2. The cut of a square mantel from a slab that is wider at the bottom of the tree than at the top. This cut squares the book for batting against the wall and makes both ends of mantel an equal width.

bricklayer knows, when he lays the first course, where the last course will end up and he can plan the thickness of the mortar to have the bricks extend to the ceiling line without having to cut the last course of brick. To do this, he must know also the thickness of the mantel. If you are using bricks, have them available before you pick out or cut your mantel because you will want to measure the thickness of the mantel to be the same as one or two or three courses of brick. This is most important if the mantel does not extend to or beyond the sides of the brick facing.

If your mantel is deep enough, you should square off the back (the edge that will butt against the wall). This is especially true if the bevel is radical, i.e., if your cut was not from the exact center of the log. By squaring off the back, the wood will lay more snugly on the brick and against the wall. When I squared mine off, I struck a chalk line along the top, 12 inches from the front, and cut it with a chain saw. See Figs. 23-2 and 23-3.

INSTALLATION FOR NEW CONSTRUCTION

When you get your bricks or stone to the height you want the mantel, let the mortar on these bricks thoroughly dry. It will set up in a few hours and, if your mantel is light, you can go to work then. Mine was heavy and I let the mortar dry for 24 hours. Set the mantel on the brick or stone and measure the ends and front. Get it exactly centered and where you want it. Prop the front with 2 × 4s and put a level on it. Make absolutely sure it is level in all directions.

I made sure the course of brick it sat on was perfectly level so that I would not have to shim the mantel. I chose not to secure the mantel to the studs in the event that I would ever want to replace it. I have it sitting on the bricks and snug against the studs on either side of the firebox. If you want to secure it to the studs, you can toenail it to them or you can put angle braces from the studs to the

Fig. 23-3. Shows the back squared off and the snug fit against the wall. The bricks are snug against the studs.

178

Fig. 23-4. The bricks are flat on the mantel. A 3″ overhang of the mantel is shown beyond the brick wall.

mantel and that should hold it. This is necessary if you intend to use paneling above instead of brick or stone.

In my "overkill" fashion, I put angle iron braces on each side, secured them to the studs with lag bolts, but did not screw or bolt them to the mantel. I put these in to hold the wood very secure when I was working on the rest of the brick work above the mantel. It was insurance that, if I kick the supporting 2 × 4s down (which I did), the mantel wouldn't tilt and ruin my mortar joints in the brick work that was not yet dry on the courses above it.

Lay the rest of the bricks or stone on top of the wood. I put the bricks directly on the wood with no mortar between the brick and the wood. Because my mantel extended beyond the brick on each side, I had no problem worrying about the courses matching. If yours does not extend to the end of the brick work, this will dictate whether you will use mortar between the bricks and the mantel or not. The courses on top of the mantel will have to match those on the side of it. Another determining factor will be where you want the top of the last course to be. You always have that half inch between the wood and the brick to play with. See Fig. 23-4.

REPLACING A MANTEL

If you want to replace an existing mantel with a free-form piece, it could be easy or difficult depending upon the construction you have. If the existing mantel is merely sitting on top of the brick and there is no brick above it, replacing it should be a piece of cake. But if you replace a thin mantel with a heavy or a wider piece, you had better secure it to the wall. There are a couple of ways to do this.

One way to do this is to remove the paneling above the brick work and place a couple of rather strong, steel angle braces on the studs and extending out right at the top of brick. In order to get the paneling back on the wall smoothly, you will have to chisel in little of the 2 × 4 and sink the angle iron into it so that the surfaces remain constant. Bolt the angle into the 2 × 4 with lag bolts and then replace the paneling. The parts sticking out above the bricks will hold the mantle piece. For a smooth job, you can even chisel out the bottom of the mantel so that it fits over the angle iron and the angle iron will not show.

If you want to replace the mantel piece on a solid brick wall, the old mantel having been supported by a couple of brick pedestals built into the wall, you probably should secure the new mantel in a little more sturdy way. The way to do this is to fasten a new mantel piece to the brick by two or three hunks of iron pipe or steel rod extending into the mantel piece and into the brick wall. Iron pipe, about 1 inch in diameter, should do the job.

Your accurate measurements from here on are important if you want the holes in the wall and in the mantel to line up. Plan the

Fig. 23-5. A 3″ brick pedestal below the mantel. With a mantel as big as this—10½′ long and 6″ thick—the pedestal would be inadequate for total support. It was installed merely for decorative value.

Fig. 23-6. When the bark was removed, worm holes were exposed. The face was hand sanded lightly and cleaned. An Early American stain was applied lightly and "quickly" so as not to allow it to penetrate the holes. This accentuated the "worminess" of the wood.

outside pipes to be in the wall at some point outside the firebox area, if possible. You do not want to punch through the upper firewall area and get in the way of the operation of the damper.

If you have to go into this area, be careful not to go any deeper than the depth of the brick or stone that you have in the face. Decide where you want the mantel and about where you want the pipes. An accurate measurement here is important. Define the center of the mantel (the center from each end, and from top and bottom). Measure from the center to the point toward each end. Keep your pipe at least 1 foot from the end of the mantel and 2 feet if your mantel is long enough. Measure the corresponding dimensions on the wall working off the center point of the firebox. Make sure your marks on the wall are level. Check with a line level. If they are off, your mantel will slant downhill.

Decide how deep you will go into the wall. Let's assume 4 inches. Use a star drill that is the same size as the pipe you will use. Go into the wall and make sure you go in straight and a full 4 inches deep. With a drill, drill into the mantel; be careful to keep the hole straight. Use a dowel hole guide if you have one. Go into the wood exactly as far as you predetermined. Let's say 6 inches. Now cut the pipe about ½ inch short of your combined lengths.

If the fit in the wall is not absolutely snug, you can fill the hole with a little cement, mixed rather wet, and hammer it into the wall. Be careful not to bugger up the end of the pipe that you are banging on. If the pipe has threads on the end, you can put a nut on the end and hold a piece of 2 × 4 when you hit it. Remove the nut when the pipes are in place. Line up the mantel piece. Have a couple of people hold it. And again, using the 2 × 4 across the front, bang it home. Don't ding up the free-form edge.

Another method of installation is to make two or three brackets to hold the mantel. You can make those brackets out of the same type of wood that the mantel is made from and the style is your decision. Attach these by the pipe method or by drilling holes in the brick with the star drill and filling them with wooden dowels. Cut the dowels flush with the wall and then use lag bolts through the bracket into these dowels to hold the brackets in place. Secure the mantel to the brackets. This method will not be adequate if the mantel is too heavy. See Figs. 23-5 and 23-6.

Chapter 24

Wall Paneling

Paneling a room with free-form boards will not be suitable for every room. Decide just how much of the free-form panelling you want to use and where. If you cover every square inch of the walls with free-form panelling, the room might look like the inside of a large packing crate. But if the room is broken up with another wall covering, and the free-form panelling is done tastefully, the room can be a show place of art and craft as well as warm and comfortable. As with all use of wood, you have to decide whether you want rough cut, sanded natural finish, stained, varnished, high gloss or satin. Because you are going with "natural" wood, you should consider that the finish you are using be one that will enhance or accentuate the naturalness rather than decorate it or obliterate it.

CHOOSING THE WOOD

The easiest boards to install are straight ones. I had mine cut from rather straight pine trees. I had them cut ½" thick. I chose this width so as to give them more body as well as get the most out of each log. Crooked boards or those that have a radical edge are interesting, but eventually they will have to butt against the straightedge board or a board with a different contour. This could produce a rather large space between the panels and would look awkward.

Boards cut from a crooked tree will all have somewhat the same contour. They can be effectively used on a small wall where they will cover the entire wall. Examples are the wall of a closet that extends out into a room or the wall behind a bar. Unless you have a short wall, avoid using irregularly fit pieces. None of your pieces will be perfectly straight, but that's what gives the wall its special appearance.

NEW CONSTRUCTION

I started to work up some paneling at the point where I had the shell of an add-on room finished. Stud walls, exterior siding, roofing, flooring, and insulation were complete and all windows and doors installed. In other words, the complete shell was finished. On the inside, the only things not done, before the paneling, were sanding the floor and installing the wiring. All the wire was strung and the outlet and switch boxes were installed. You can put the paneling in before the finished floor is laid if you prefer. My starting point was the bare studs.

The first thing I did was put horizontal nailers between each stud at about half way up the wall. See Fig. 24-1. Some of my knowledgeable friends thought these nailers were unnecessary. But my thinking was that the boards for the paneling were possibly not completely dry yet and I wanted them secure on the top, middle, and bottom to prevent warping. In putting in these braces, I staggered them so that I could nail in through the stud to each one and not have to toenail them.

The next thing I did was to panel the walls with some old and varied colored panelling. I put the grooved finished side against the studs and left the back show. I did this so that the small spaces in between the boards would not show the insulation behind them. I left the back side showing because I thought it would take a dark stain better than the glossy side.

I wasn't too particular about the installation. I used odd-shaped and sized pieces and placed them together to cover the whole wall. I tacked each piece top and bottom, and I put a few nails in each stud so that I would know where the studs and nailers were without remeasuring each one later. The paneling, by the way, extended from the floor to butt against the 2-×-6 ceiling joists.

Now for the boards themselves. Start in a corner and work down the wall. Pick a board with a rather straight edge. Now you have a choice. Put it up as is and butt the free edge into the corner or cut the free edge off the side and put a straight edge in the corner. If the adjoining wall in that corner will be paneled, I suggest using the straight edge. If not, see how the free-form edge in the corner appeals to you.

185

Fig. 24-1. The placement of braces or cross pieces of 2 × 4 between studs to be used as nailers for the free-form paneling.

Because there is not yet a ceiling, you can allow your boards to extend a few inches above the top of the wall if your joints do not get in the way. As you put up the first board, decide which way you want the free edge to flow. Do you want the board visible or turned around so that the bevel moves from the outside of the board into the wall behind it? The choice as to whether you want the bevel showing or not is a matter of preference. Keep in mind that, in the spaces left between the boards, you might want to put a contrasting stain to show off, more obviously, the free edge. When you decide to put the board up, tack it at the top and bottom. You can nail it tight after you see what a few boards look like when they are up.

Select the second board. All the bevels go the same way as the first one that you put up. As long as the edges are fairly straight, the spaces in between should not be too large. If there is a protruding knot or edge, cut it off.

Here is the way to do that. Pry the previous board loose and place the new board against the wall with the knot extending behind. Position it as you would want it on the wall. Mark the piece with a pencil and cut it with a sabre saw. Another method of doing this, is to lay the boards on the floor and match them before you put them up. If you have a few feet extra, with regards to the length of the boards, you can move it up or down as they lay on the floor to get a better match. Another point to keep in mind is that the boards you use are, more likely than not, wider at one end than the other. It might be necessary to position some of the boards "up side down" in order to keep them running straight on the wall.

Another good idea is to stagger the boards as to width. Because every log will give you wide boards out of the middle, as well as narrow ones from the outer cuts, you would be conscious of varying the width as you go along. Work your way down the wall.

Your next problem will be when you hit a window. The best thing to do is to cut out the board bordering the window and keep a straight edge all the way around the window. I made a straight edge even with the 2 × 4s that surrounded the window because I wanted to put molding around the inside of the window from the same wood that I used for paneling. Work your way around the room and frame the window out later. As you go under and over a window, try to get the last bottom and top boards to end up about the same distance from the side of the window and a few inches short of it. This will enable you to use one solid board for the next piece that will extend again from the floor to the ceiling, and have the notch cut out of it to give the straight edge to the window.

Fig. 24-2. The paneling in a corner. Note that the corner has straight edges.

If you have a sliding-glass door, you can get away with a free edge on each side. If part sticks out a bit, it will not interfere with the opening and closing of the door. You can tack it up and see if you like it. Where you have a door that opens out you must be more careful. I suggest a straight edge there.

Fig. 24-3. A closeup of the corner. Note that ceiling plasterboard has no molding.

Continue past your door to the corner. The corner board takes a bit of extra fitting. Here's one way to do it. Assuming you are working left to right, head for the corner at your right hand. After you fit your next to last board and cut it lengthwise to size, set it in place but don't nail it. As you stand holding it in place, measure from some point at the top of it and on the left hand side of it, across the board and across the space right to the corner. Do the same thing at the bottom. Your measurements will be different but that's OK.

Take the board down and lay it on the floor and fit the last board to it. Then cut it to the proper height. With the boards fitted together on the floor, measure again from the *same spot* that you previously measured. Mark the top measurement on the last board and then do the same at the bottom. Strike a chalk line from the top to the bottom of this last board. This will be the straightedge that will fit in the corner perfectly (provided your measurements were accurate). Fit the two boards in and nail. You can work in either direction; just reverse the measurements. See Figs. 24-2 and 24-3.

If you intend to turn the corner with paneling, take your next board and cut a straightedge on the left-hand side. Waste as little paneling as possible. Fit this panel into the corner and nail it. On these corner cuts, it would be wise to use a 2-×-4 saw guide clamped to your board for an even cut. This insures a nice fit and eliminates the need for corner molding when you might not want to use it. I suggest that you don't use molding if it is at all possible.

WINDOW MOLDING

Assuming that you used a straight cut around the windows with the paneling even with the 2-×-4 structure of the window, you are ready to install the molding. Here we go with your choices again. You could use a free edge all the way around or you could use the same wood as your paneling, but with the free edge cut off. You could use the straight cut for the top and sides and free edge for a sill. I like this idea because I consider the amount of free edge between each board just about enough. Also, if you use straight cuts for the top and sides of your window, you can use the rest of the board and not waste as much. I suggest that you cut both styles for a window; use the free edge all the way around and the straight cut. Set them in place and see which you like. See Fig. 24-4.

To set your sill first, you must figure out just where the sill will butt against the window. This will depend on what type of window you have (aluminum with a bottom well, tract, wooden). You can figure out where your sill will stop by a close look at the bottom of the window.

Fig. 24-4. A closeup of a window sill. The sill carries a free-form edge and extends both out and to the side of frame. On this window the side pieces were cut square and flush.

191

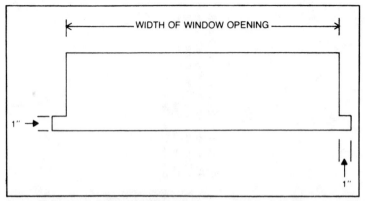

Fig. 24-5. A diagram of a sill. The width and depth are determined by the dimensions of the frame and the amount of overhang you want. This sketch indicates a 1″ overhang in front and sides.

Figure out just how far out your sill will extend beyond the paneling below the window. Its a matter of preference. Set a piece up and move it in and out to the point where you like it.

Keep in mind if you want to put a small piece of molding under the sill (free-edge or straight-cut molding from the same wood). If you want to use molding here, estimate the depth of the sill with a piece of molding held on or tacked in place. I had the sill extend about an inch over the paneling.

You might want to make your sill a thicker stock than your paneling. If the paneling boards are ½″ thick, you could make your sill a full inch. I did this only because I had a few boards that were thicker than all the rest. When the sawmill cuts the logs, they work in from each side. When the middle piece is too thin to hold the clamps, you get whatever the thickness happens to be.

Make sure it is not so thick that it will go too high on your window frame and inhibit the windows from opening or that it will extend above the glass. No matter what thickness, you will want the sill to extend about an inch on each side beyond the width of the window. This too is a matter of choice. If you want the overhang on each side, cut the sill 2 inches wider than the opening in your paneling.

Measure the depth of the window well; that means from where the sill will butt against the window to the outside edge of the panelling. Add your inch here and, with the 2 inches you added to the width, you have the dimensions of your sill. You will have to cut out a piece on each end of the sill to make it fit. See Fig. 24-5. Fasten it with finishing nails and use glue if you think it is necessary.

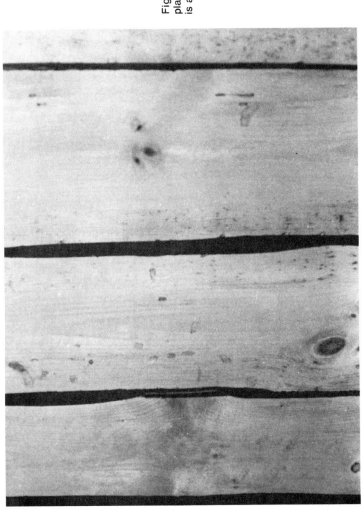

Fig. 24-6. These boards were planed only (not sanded). The finish is a semigloss clear polyurethane.

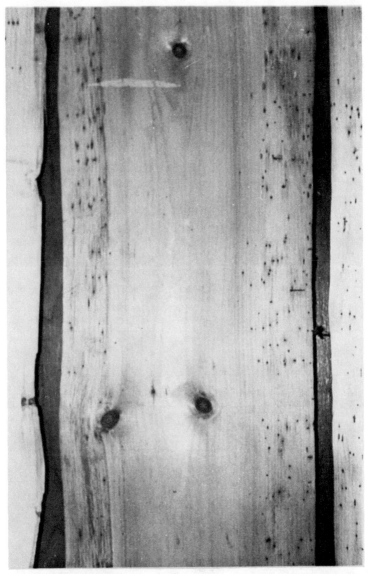

Fig. 24-7. The rustic look.

Next put in your top piece. Make it the exact width of the opening and have it extend to the outside edge of paneling but no farther. Nail and glue it in place. Put the side pieces in next. After they are nailed in place, run a belt sander down the edges of the boards to make sure that they are even with the paneling.

FINISHING

The next step is to do whatever you have in mind with the spaces between the boards. Usually they contrast with the tone of the paneling. Because my paneling was light, I used a walnut stain between the boards. When you have finished the room "between the boards," run a belt sander over the paneling to smooth out all rough edges. Clean off any dirty spots that turn up. Now you are ready to apply the stain or finish. If the boards are rough and just the way they came from the saw mill, be careful with the belt sander. You do not want any smooth streaks in the rustic look. See Figs. 24-6 and 24-7.

Your room will be an unusual combination of natural wood blended to a fine and finished wall covering. It will be something to be proud of and a conversation piece to say the least.

Chapter 25

Frame Repair

In Chapter 6, on building sofas, I suggested that you take an old couch, strip it down to the frame, remove the arms, repair the frame where necessary and then build up a new free-form couch from that. This chapter provides additional information regarding repair and even some tips on restyling.

The frame determines the general shape, size, and style of your couch or chair. It is always worth your extra time and effort to repair and strengthen a frame. The finest looking piece of furniture is really no good if it falls apart. In replacing broken wooden parts or firming up a frame with other wood parts, try and use a medium-hard wood with a straight grain and no knots. Use dowels or screws for all connections. The wood that is hidden within the frame area and not seen need not be clean or sanded, but it has to be good wood and not junk.

All joints should be glued along with the dowels or screws that hold them together. Occasionally, angle brackets or nuts and bolts are practical for fastening joints. Whatever combination you use never use nails. Nails are unreliable and impractical for furniture frames. They will quickly work loose under any twisting motion.

If your furniture will be put to exceptionally hard use, little children diving on it and the like, I suggest that rather than using carpenter's glue for the joint connections, you use a hot glue, a resin, or a hide glue that will be much more tolerant of stress than white glue. I usually use dowel and glue joints for repairing frames. They are probably the easiest and they are among the strongest.

Make sure the dowel diameter is never more than half of the dimension of the surface that the dowel will be in. Two or more dowels are stronger than one, and especially if they can be placed in a staggered position. Glue blocks should also be used whenever possible on all weight-bearing joints. Make sure that the glue block sits snugly and that it is glued well in as many corners of the frame as possible. See Figs. 25-1 and 25-2.

Spacings between the slats on the seat of the couch or the back must never be more than 24 inches apart (though it can be less). All these slates should be glued and doweled with at least two dowels per joint. Most frame repair consists of regluing and reenforcing weak joints, and repairing broken slats and legs. Where a joint has to be reglued, and the dowel has pulled out—as long as the dowel itself is intact and nothing is split or broken—you can clean all the old glue off and reglue it, clamp it firm, and leave the clamps on until the glue is dried.

In some cases, the dowels will have to be replaced. Saw the dowel off flat with the joint, redrill, and insert a new dowel where the slats have to be replaced. Saw them off even with the frame,

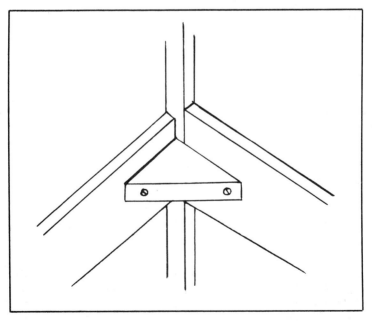

Fig. 25-1. A solid glue block is used to brace a corner joint. This is secured by both glue and screws. Screws can be inserted through the blind side if those parts will be hidden or covered.

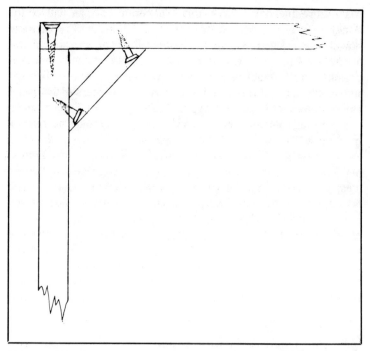

Fig. 25-2. This is a variation of the glue block. It is used where the corner joint is not a perfect 90° angle or has an offset. This type can be found in commercial frames even in "perfect" corners because they are more economical to install.

redrill, and redowel the new piece in place. You can add metal angle braces or corner glue blocks to all the joints to beef them up.

Most legs can be easily repaired; this is especially true for those that will not be seen. They can be completely taken off and replaced with casters, they can be taken off and used as a pattern to cut a new piece or a new leg from a 2 × 4, or they can be replaced by the very short commercial screw-on legs. If the contour along the top of the back is not to your liking, you can cut it off and replace it with a straight piece of wood (dowel and glue each joint).

Removing the arms is no problem. This is most easily done by sawing off the armboard and arm stump holding it. Sometimes the whole side can be removed without the couch completely collapsing. In other words, the style can be changed by reshaping it to conform better with the free-form wood.

SUPPORTING THE SEAT CONSTRUCTION

If the springs and braces in a couch or chair seat assembly or even the back assembly are completely shot, you can replace the whole structure with a solid plywood base. Remove the braces and the springs and insert another rail on the inside of the existing seat rail to support the plywood (glue blocks might be sufficient). Cover the complete back or the complete seat with plywood. I would suggest at least ⅜″ plywood. If you use anything thicker, your piece will become very heavy. If you can tolerate this, by all means do it.

On top of the plywood, the back or the seat will be most easily finished with foam. When using foam—over a solid wood surface—you must allow for the escape of air when the foam is compressed. If the foam will be covered with a porous fabric, you must have two ½″ holes per square foot of wood surface. Block off the square footage with a pencil on your seat and make sure you drill ½″ holes throughout the base at two per square foot.

If you cover the foam with a "nonbreathing" or airtight material such as vinyl or a synthetic leather, you must have four ½″ holes per square foot of wood surface. These are the minimum desirable venting surfaces in order to prevent a "whooshing" sound of escaping air when you sit on the cushion or a cushion that stays compressed because of a slow air return.

SPRINGS AND SPRING SUPPORTS

Examine the springs in the seat and back carefully. Make sure that they are all tied to the other springs. Make sure that the contour along the top of the springs is even. If the springs are extended and erratic, it might be better to replace the whole system with plywood or to get a new couch frame or chair frame and start all over.

The bottom support of the spring can be easily replaced if it is a fabric or webbing support. When replacing these, make sure that the new webbing is put in exactly as the old webbing was and tied or sewed in the same places. When replacing fabric webbing, there is a stretcher that is used in frame building that is made for pulling the webbing taut. As an amateur furniture maker, you probably do not have one. I replaced webbing one time by putting two small pieces of wood on each side and clamping it firmly with a vise grip. As I tugged on the vise grip, someone else tacked the webbing into place when it was taut. You can makeshift this procedure as long as you are not doing too much of it. If your job is big, I suggest that you find a webbing stretcher.

When putting on new webbing, make sure that you do not cut it so short that you don't have room to hold it while you stretch it. Make sure that you fold over 1½″ of the free webbing at the end where you tack it to the frame. Pull the webbing taut, tack it into place, fold over the 1½" and then tack it with about seven tacks per end that are staggered. When you tack webbing to the rail, do not bring it out to the absolute end of the rail; recess it about ½" from the rail edge.

When you pull your webbing taut, if it distorts the frame in any way, that is an indication that you must put more braces in the frame. By all means do so. When you have completed your webbing, each spring must be stitched to it. Stitching twine and needles are sold for this job. Any stitch that will hold them secure and will not come loose is satisfactory. Before you take it apart, study the way and the places in which springs are stitched to the webbing. Usually each spring is sewn in four places.

Many other types of coil springs or flat, metal-strip springs are found in furniture. Make sure that they don't sag and that they are fastened securely to the frame. If you are satisfied with the looks of the spring construction, you can proceed to building your couch or chair. When your construction is completed, the springs must be covered with fabric to keep the stuffing materials from falling into them. Use heavy burlap to cover all springs. Cut the burlap large enough to cover all the springs and stretch them from rail to rail. Pull it taut and tack it to the rails. It would be a good idea to double the burlap around the edges to give it more strength under the tacks. Then stitch the burlap to each of the coil springs.

FOAM

Foam rubber or synthetic foam are probably the best materials for an amateur upholsterer to work with because they don't require the tools or the expertise that fiber materials require. Foam comes in different densities and they are branded as extra soft, soft, medium, firm, and extra firm. Most fabric stores do not carry all the densities. The best results are obtained by layers of different density foam rather than one 3-inch cushion of medium or soft.

Too soft foam will not hold its shape. Too hard foam may be uncomfortable. A layer of firm density should be used under a soft-density foam. Even three layers could be effective. The bottom layer could be 2-inch firm, the middle layer could possibly be 1-inch medium, and the top layer could be 1-inch very soft. Many upholsterers cover their foam with muslin or a cotton-felt padding on top before the final upholstery material is applied.

CUTTING AND GLUING FOAM

The best knife to use for cutting foam is an electric carving knife, but any serrated edge knife will do the job. When foam is glued, as layers should be, the best adhesive is the one suggested by the manufacturer of that particular type of foam. The wrong kind of adhesive or cheap glue can dry or crack and will become ineffective in the long run. Foam adhesive comes in spray cans and in liquid. Follow the directions on the container.

FINAL UPHOLSTERY

The combination of the upholstery and the free form wood will determine the outcome of your project. You must use the upholstery material very carefully in order to accentuate and not detract from the free-form design that you put so much work and time into. Before you decide on a fabric cover, you should decide on a style and color. Try to visualize how they will match the tone of the wood that you have used. Upholstery material comes in three weights: heavy, medium, and light.

I would caution against covering a couch or chair with anything but upholstery material because other materials just do not hold up and it would be a shame to have all that work be short lived. The couches and chairs that I have made have been very plain. I stretched the material around the back and stapled it to the frame. The cushions I did not even begin to attempt. I had the foam covered by a professional. It did not make sense to me for the few extra dollars to wreck what I consider a beautiful piece of furniture with sloppy cushions. And sloppy would have been the best I could have done with them. When you are completely finished, it would be a good idea to apply a dust cover. Turn the furniture over and tack the material to the rail on the bottom. For a dust cover, a stiff black cambric is usually used.

I know people who have made beautiful furniture and then had it completely upholstered by a professional. If you can afford this, it certainly has a pleasing outcome. I know other people who have made furniture and covered the foam with a "throw" and it has certainly been both presentable and functional as well as very inexpensive. In some cases, it might be possible to reupholster the back of the sofa or a chair and then recover the cushions with your material.

Glossary

bar clamp—*See* furniture clamp.

bevel—*See* chamfer.

brace and bit—A hand drill (brace) with the drill (bit) having a square shaft.

butt—Two boards or surfaces being joined together at right angles.

butt hinge—A door or cabinet hinge that simply folds together (no offset).

C-clamp—A C-shaped metal clamp with a screw-type tightening device used to hold two pieces of glued wood until complete adhesion has taken place.

carriage bolt—Has a round smooth head and a square protrusion below the head to hold in wood while a nut is tightened.

chamfer—To cut, plane or sand away the edge of a board to an angle.

chuck—The end part of a drill, electric or hand, that holds the cutting bit. This is usually tightened and loosened with a chuck key.

Colonial—A furniture style that is very functional. It shows some evidence of European influence. Takes its name from the colonization period of American history.

counter punch—Round metal tool about 3″ long with point and blunt head used for driving finish nails below surface.

countersink—Where a larger hole is drilled a short distance over a smaller hole in order to bury the screw head below the surface or to place a dowel on top of it.

dado—A U-shaped slot or groove cut in one surface to accept and support another board at right angles.

dowel—A sized round hardwood length of wood measured by the diameter. A ½″ dowel has a ½″ diameter.

Early American—A style of furniture that contains much detail with intricate moldings and lathe turnings.

expansion bit—A drill bit that can be adjusted to bore different size holes.

finish nail—A nail that comes in many sizes and has a small head that can be driven beneath the surface with a counter punch. The hole can then be filled and sanded smooth.

free edge (free form)—Boards with the bark or at least the natural edge of the tree intact. When used in furniture, some of the free edge (or even the bark) is left natural.

furniture clamp (bar clamp)—Has a spread up to 8 feet. Used to hold furniture when it is being glued.

half-lap joint—When two boards are to be joined at right angles, half the thickness of each is removed to give a larger and stronger fastening surface.

kickboard—The facing board along the front of a sofa or chair. It is between the cushion and the floor.

millwork—Used to describe work done in woodworking plants (and sometimes lumber mills). Finished products like molding or cabinets or semifinished work as planning and sanding boards.

mitre—A right angle made by cutting each board on a 45-degree angle.

mitre box—A box with saw guides to insure proper 45-degree cuts.

mortise—A complete hole or a hole part way through to receive a tenon. The female half of the joint.

nail block—An extra block of wood installed to reinforce a joint.

pegged—Hardwood dowels are used to join wooden parts. They are also used to cover countersink screws to give the pegged look.

Pioneer—A style of furniture that is heavy, rustic, functional and unadorned. Named after the style of furniture used by the early settlers.

plumb—Perpendicular to the floor and level in all directions. A plumb bob is a weight on a string used to measure perpendicularity.

protractor—An instrument for measuring angles.

pumice—A powdered form of lava used in fine sanding.

rabbet—An L-shaped groove cut into the edge of a board so it can accept another board at a right angle in a recessed manor.

relief—A carved wood or molded plastic that is glued to a flat wood surface.

router—A hand-held electrical tool that turns assorted cutting bits at about 27,000 rpm's and is used for rabbets, mortises, various molded edges, or gouging out lettering in signs.

Shaker—A style of furniture that is austerely plain. It is mainly made of pine and maple. The name was taken from a religious sect circa 1776.

shim—A small piece of wood used between two other pieces to hold them apart. Used in leveling or aligning.

slab—A lengthwise slice from a log. In this book the slabs referred to have the natural edge in tact.

stretcher—The wooden board used to hold the legs of a table or bench at a desired distance and angle from each other. It adds support and strength to the piece.

T-square—A tool used to measure right angles.

tack rag—Cloth dampened with varnish used to remove dust before finishing.

tenon—The male part of a joint. This projection fits into the female mortise.

trestle table—Early American style table. Takes its name from a trestle bridge; a main horizontal beam fixed at each end by columns (or legs). This trestle supports the tabletop.

white glue (carpenters' glue)—A polyvinyl adhesive used in bonding wood.

Index

Index